HOW
TO
BOIL
AN
EGG

BY

ROSE CARRARINI

HOW TO BOIL AN EGG

POACH ONE, SCRAMBLE ONE
FRY ONE, BAKE ONE, STEAM ONE

ROSE BAKERY

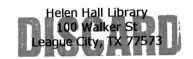

INTRODUCTION

Like most people, I have never paid eggs any special attention or considered them particularly worth talking about, but just taken them for granted. So, could I, with real sincerity, suggest that their role in the kitchen is as important as that of fruit and vegetables, grains and pulses (legumes), fish and meat? As soon as I started to think about that, the answer was obvious. Without eggs, Rose Bakery's list of foods would be greatly diminished and compromised and our pastry section would be almost non-existent. In fact, we use eggs every day as an essential ingredient in cakes, cookies and quiches, a partner for bacon, a thickener for creams and sauces and many other uses. The humble and unassuming egg is, indeed, an essential ingredient.

When we opened the first Rose Bakery in Paris in 2002 our aim was to serve simple, fresh food, using as much organic produce as possible and selecting the best-quality ingredients we could find. We particularly wanted to promote the use of vegetables and grains, but at the same time the provenance of our dairy, meat, fish and eggs was extremely important. The origin of food matters very much to me and I believe that this strong viewpoint has encouraged the trust our customers have placed in Rose Bakery. This is simply the way I live and I couldn't honestly deal with food in any other way. The response to this approach was, to say the least, gratifying, as we soon found ourselves with queues snaking out the door of our small premises, particularly as we were located in an area already richly supplied with pâtisseries and cafés. Rose Bakery started in Paris on the rue des Martyrs and has since opened on rue Debelleyme in the Marais, as well as in the art gallery Maison Rouge in the tenth arrondissement. There are also branches in London, Tokyo and Seoul.

For me, eggs are the perfect example of a simple, natural food. People have been eating them since ancient times, whether baked, fried, poached, boiled, pickled, blended in breads and cakes, raw and even painted. The increasingly sophisticated ways in which they are used seem to me to be a question of trial and error and, most importantly, personal taste, and this is something I will touch on again and again as it is so fundamental to cooking eggs. From the start we wanted Rose Bakery to be a creative place and we are still experimenting

{ Hen's Egg }

all these years later. This is especially true with eggs, whether they are taking the starring role as in Eggs Baked in Dashi *(see page 34)*, are served very simply as in Egg Salad with Arame & Rice *(see page 84)* or form part of a list of ingredients as in Chocolate & Orange Polenta Cake *(see page 103)*. So with this book I have decided to give eggs the attention they deserve and my collection of recipes will show that this everyday ingredient should be highly valued for its versatility and creative potential. Consequently, my recipes include all kinds of dishes for different times of day: family favourites for breakfast, such as Egg in the Middle *(see page 30)*, my own versions of chawanmushi, or Japanese savoury custard, *(see pages 77-78)* for lunch, and delicious cakes and desserts for tea – or any time of day – such as a contemporary twist on a classic with Soy Crème Caramel *(see page 112)*.

We make about 35 different cakes at Rose Bakery and, apart from the vegan recipes, they all need eggs, either whole or just the whites. They are used for the meringues in our pavlovas and Eton messes, are crucial in the fillings for our quiches and act as setting agents for our crème caramels and bread and butter puddings. In fact, every week we sell hundreds of items that need eggs and I can't imagine what we'd do without them, especially as our pastry section is half our business. On several occasions I can remember running out of eggs and you wouldn't believe the panic... So, for us, the value of these humble little things is immense.

Eggs are one of the most nutritious foods we can eat, especially the yolks. They are also one of the most easily available and great value for money. I always buy organic free-range eggs. This method of farming chickens means that they are kept in humane conditions and allowed to prosper in a sustainable manner. They are reared outdoors without being crushed by other birds, are not routinely given antibiotics and are fed a healthy diet. Organic eggs come from healthier hens and, compared to other eggs, are richer in essential nutrients. So, why would we even think of buying other types of eggs? Of course financial concerns can play a large part in our choices, but I would rather cut back on something else in order to buy good eggs.

The egg is nature's multi-vitamin and mineral supplement, and is full of protein. Protein is essential for optimal growth in children and body repair in adults. It is also essential for maintaining muscles, a healthy immune system, a stable nervous system and beautiful hair, skin and nails. Eggs contain almost all the vitamins except vitamin C. They are rich in vitamin A, which is good for healthy eyes and skin, B group vitamins for energy, E for beautiful skin and a healthy heart, D and K for strong bones. They also contain a wealth of minerals, including iodine, phosphorus, sulphur, zinc, iron, selenium and potassium. Eggs are a major source of choline, which protects the liver and is an important nutrient for pregnant women.

A few years ago I was diagnosed with high blood cholesterol levels, in spite of my healthy diet. At the time I was told that eating eggs raises blood cholesterol levels, so I stopped eating them. It is a complex issue but the latest research indicates that eggs do not cause or add to any blood cholesterol problems, and may even help promote general health if eaten as part of a balanced diet. There are also no real limits to how many eggs we can eat a day, but I suspect a moderate two or three is sensible.

Some of the recipes in this book are classic and simple while others are more complex and use unusual ingredients. I want to show the many and varied ways we cook our eggs at Rose Bakery and illustrate how we like to be creative with them. I hope, too, to encourage you to cook them more often. I have tried not to cheat and simply give lots of recipes for wonderful vegetable dishes with just the addition of an egg on top. The eggs in the following recipes are an integral and important part, of the dish and without them the recipe would be meaningless. The only exception – there's always one – is ratatouille, which I think goes well with most foods, but especially with eggs. Eggs are really one of the only foods that are perfect for morning, noon, afternoon, evening and even bedtime.

TIPS, TECHNIQUES AND INGREDIENTS

Tips for Cooking with Eggs

We always use organic eggs and they are usually a size medium (US large) – the average weight is 50 g (2 ounces) and about 12 per cent of this is shell. As a general rule, organic eggs come from hens that have been humanely treated and have spent some time foraging outdoors. Their diet tends to make the shells much easier to peel off than those of intensively reared chickens. Although brown eggs look especially appetizing, they do not differ nutritionally from white eggs. The colour depends solely on the particular breed of hen. Similarly, the colour of the yolk is no indication of quality.

Storing eggs

The best way to keep eggs fresh is in the refrigerator, where they may be kept for up to 3 weeks, but you should still check the 'use-by' date before using them. You can also check the freshness by placing an egg in a bowl or glass and covering it with cold water. If it stays horizontal, the egg is very fresh; if it tilts slightly upward, it may be as much as 10 days old; if it floats vertically, it is stale. The shell is porous so it should not be washed before storage as this will make it permeable to smells such as garlic. Keep eggs in the refrigerator, pointed ends downward. If you need eggs for making cakes, I recommend taking them out of the refrigerator at least 1 hour before using and letting them come to room temperature.

Separating eggs

Tap the egg gently on a hard surface or on the edge of a glass bowl and a crack will appear. Place your thumbs either side of the crack, carefully prise the egg open and you should end up with more or less equal halves. Tip the yolk from one half-shell to the other several times, letting the white drain into a bowl. Remember that if you get even the smallest trace of egg yolk in the whites, they will not foam up, however long you whisk them.

Raw eggs

Raw or very lightly cooked eggs are best avoided by infants, the elderly, pregnant women, convalescents and those with a suppressed immune system.

Techniques

Measuring ingredients

Some recipes, such as those for pastries and cakes, require very accurate measurements. Electronic scales are most accurate for weighing dry ingredients; if you are using spring balance scales, make sure that the pointer is at zero before you start. A heatproof glass jug or measuring cup is ideal for measuring larger quantities of liquid. Check the quantity at eye level. Small quantities of dry and liquid ingredients are measured by teaspoons and tablespoons. Always use a set of proper measuring spoons – usually $1/4$, $1/2$, $3/4$ and 1 teaspoon, plus 1 tablespoon – rather than tableware spoons (1 teaspoon = 5 ml; 1 tablespoon = 15 ml). Scoop up dry ingredients, such as cornflour (cornstarch), then level with the blade of a knife. Use and level measuring cups in the same way. Do not measure small quantities of liquids directly over a mixing bowl, as a slip of the hand can be disastrous. Use either cups or metric measurements; do not combine them.

Oven temperatures

Allow up to 15 minutes for the oven to preheat and do not put a dish, especially a cake, in the oven until it has reached the required temperature. Ovens vary, so use your judgement and knowledge of your own oven for timings. The best thing to do is check your dish at intervals from 10–15 minutes before the end of the suggested cooking time just to be sure that it will not over-cook. Bear in mind that fan-assisted ovens cook more rapidly than conventional ovens so either adjust the temperature or reduce the cooking time – check the manufacturer's handbook.

Bain maries

There are two types of bain marie: one for use in the oven and one for on top of the stove. In the oven we use a roasting pan that is at least 4 cm / $1\frac{1}{2}$ inches deep. We put the dish or dishes we want to bake or steam into the pan, pour in warm water to come one-third or halfway up the side of the dish, cover the roasting tray with foil and bake. For the stove top, put the ingredients – chocolate to be melted or egg yolks and sugar to be beaten – into a heatproof bowl and set over a pan of barely simmering water. Do not let the base of the bowl touch the surface of the water. Double boilers are also available.

Pans

We generally use cast-iron frying pans or skillets at the restaurant, but a non-stick pan will do just as well. For scrambled eggs we use a new type of non-stick pan that is more 'eco-friendly' but the egg doesn't come away so easily. We always use a wooden spoon to stir scrambled eggs, as it's much gentler.

Ingredients

Using organically farmed produce has always been important to me, partly because I want to avoid the risks of chemical residues as far as possible. Equally important is knowing that the food itself and the land where it has been raised have been well nurtured.

Butter

We have always used an unsalted butter called Lescure for everything. It is perfect for pastry, as the water content is very low, and it is really good for making cakes too. We never use salted butter. Even if you prefer salted butter, it is better to use unsalted for sweet baking and for greasing baking pans as it is less likely to scorch.

Chocolate

The chocolate we always use is Valrhona's Guanaja 70 per cent, but Green & Black's Dark or Montezuma's Very Dark 73 per cent are among other very good brands, too.

Dashi

Made from kombu seaweed and bonito flakes, this is the type of stock most frequently used in Japan. You can make it yourself, but we use a really delicious concentrated one that we dilute. It is completely natural and found in good Japanese supermarkets. Dashi stock granules are also available. We sometimes add fresh ginger or a splash of soy sauce. It's worth experimenting to find out what suits you best.

Arame

This is a dried seaweed found in Japanese food stores. It needs to soak in warm water for about 10 minutes before using. When cooked, it has a lovely, sweet, nutty flavour and is an excellent source of calcium.

Marigold bouillon powder

We use this brand of bouillon powder as it is delicious, made from entirely natural organic produce and free from monosodium glutamate. If you don't have time to make your own stock, this is what we recommend. It is widely available from whole food stores and supermarkets.

Olive Oil

We always use Italian extra-virgin olive oil simply because I prefer the taste of Italian oils. However, other Mediterranean countries, including Spain, France and Greece, as well as California, Australia and New Zealand, produce high-quality oils, each with a distinctive flavour.

Purple Corn Powder

This powder is made by pulping the purple corn cob, which comes from South America, and then evaporating all the liquid. It has a hint of the same flavour and sweetness as its better-known golden yellow cousin. It is extremely high in health-giving antioxidants. It may be difficult to track down; it is available from my favourite wellness store, Snowsfields in London and on the internet.

Salt

We generally use Maldon sea salt, but any natural sea salt is good.

Shoyu

This is a light soy sauce from Japan. Do not substitute Chinese soy sauce as it has a much stronger flavour.

Vanilla

We use a vanilla extract that is very intense, so we only add a drop. Commercial vanilla flavourings – natural or otherwise – available from supermarkets, can be used by the teaspoon, as they are much less concentrated.

Yacón Syrup

This is a sugar substitute from South America. It is glucose-free, and does not increase blood sugar levels. We use it in a few of our cakes and desserts to make them healthier.

SIMPLY EGGS

{ Boiled Egg }

SIMPLY EGGS

Boiled Eggs
Poached Eggs
Scrambled Eggs
Fried Eggs
Omelette

SAUCES

Mayonnaise
Hollandaise Sauce
Béarnaise Sauce

There are five basic ways to cook eggs – boiled, poached, scrambled, fried and in omelettes – although there are variations on these standard techniques. Sometimes these basic ways of cooking eggs form an integral part of a recipe, such as hard-boiled eggs in Our Salad Niçoise *(see page 81)*, poached eggs in Eggs Benedict *(see page 33)*, scrambled eggs in Scrambled Eggs with Tomato *(see page 29)*, fried or poached eggs in Mashed Potatoes, Eggs & Parmesan *(see page 75)* and omelettes in Omelette Sandwich *(see page 88)*. At other times they are simply the perfect partners for other recipes, for example serving scrambled eggs with Cheddar, Leek & Curry Scones *(see page 39)* and poached or fried eggs with Rose Bakery Ratatouille *(see page 76)*. There are, of course, many other possibilities and variations, which only serves to demonstrate once again the versatility of this most useful ingredient at any time of day, whether breakfast, lunch or tea.

The right and wrong way to cook eggs is quite difficult to pin down because everyone has their own preferences and tastes. Some people like crisply fried eggs, while others prefer a softer texture and some like their eggs fried in butter, while others insist they should be cooked in oil. As for the 'perfectly' boiled egg, this can range from almost completely runny to hard-boiled. Omelettes present another area of contention and the list of preferences is almost endless. I can only tell you how we like to eat them, so you might have to adjust according to your preference. There is, however, one cardinal rule: eggs should always be cooked gently and slowly, by whatever method, as the white and yolk coagulate at well below boiling point.

The classic egg-based sauces rely on the unique properties of eggs to bind the ingredients. They make wonderful accompaniments to fish, vegetable and other dishes, and they taste much better when freshly-made.

BOILED EGGS

To cook soft-boiled eggs, bring a pan of water to a boil and, using a large spoon, gently lower the eggs into it. Time them as follows:

Small (US medium) **eggs – 3 minutes**
Medium (US large) **eggs – 4 minutes**
Large (US extra large) **eggs – 4½ minutes**

As soon as the time is up, take them out with a slotted spoon, refresh under cold water for a second, then put them into egg cups.

These timings will produce eggs with the whites just set and the yolks still soft.

To cook hard-boiled eggs, put them into a pan of cold water and bring to a boil.

Reduce the heat and simmer for 15–20 minutes, then drain off the hot water and replace with cold.

Let stand until the eggs are cool enough to shell.

In both cases, it is best to remove the eggs from the refrigerator and bring to room temperature before cooking.

POACHED EGGS

Many people are nervous about poaching eggs, and to some extent this is understandable. Success depends quite considerably on the freshness of the egg, as an old egg with a watery white will end up a disaster. Some chefs suggest pre-boiling the eggs for 30 seconds and then chilling them before breaking them into the water, but I don't find this is necessary.

Bring a pan half-filled with water to a boil and add 1 tablespoon vinegar.

Stir vigorously to create a whirlpool in the centre and immediately break an egg into the whirlpool.

Continue to stir gently for about 1½ minutes.

Lift out the egg with a slotted spoon, holding a paper towel under it to catch the excess water, then turn over onto a plate.

If the white looks a little straggly, you can trim it if you like.

Poaching one egg at a time is pretty much fail-safe but you can cook several in the same pan – just make sure that they don't touch.

SCRAMBLED EGGS

Melt a piece of butter in a pan over medium-low heat.

Meanwhile, beat 3 eggs per serving with a little salt and pepper in a bowl, then pour into the pan. If the eggs start cooking madly at once, remove the pan and lower the heat before returning it, as it is important that they cook gently.

Cook, stirring constantly, with a wooden spoon, until they are soft and creamy and keep their shape.

Under-cooked scrambled eggs that leak out across the plate are just as unappetizing as dried-up over-cooked eggs. This should be a bright yellow mound of deliciousness. If you have difficulty getting just the right texture for scrambled eggs, you might find it easier to cook them in a double boiler or bain maire (see page 11), so that the heat is very gentle.

FRIED EGGS

Heat about 1 tablespoon olive oil and a piece of butter, if you wish, in a non-stick frying pan or skillet over medium-low heat.

When the pan is hot, crack the eggs into it as gently as possible, shaking the pan slightly to prevent them from sticking. If the eggs set off a firework display of spurting oil, remove the pan from the heat, as the oil has become too hot, and reduce the heat before returning the pan. The eggs should start setting slowly.

As soon as the whites are set and the yolks are securely held, remove them with a spatula, draining off any excess oil on paper towels, and serve immediately.

OMELETTE

The important point is that an omelette should be the simplest thing, nothing grand and showy. If they are to be filled, use only small amounts of simple ingredients such as herbs, cheese, ham or bacon, tomato or mushrooms. The filling should not detract from the eggs and be tucked inside, out of sight.

Serves 1

Heat a 25 cm (10 inch) frying pan or skillet, preferably non-stick.

Lightly mix 3 eggs with a fork in a bowl. Add a piece of butter or a tablespoon of olive oil to the pan.

When the pan is hot, pour in the eggs, which should immediately start to set. Tilt the pan toward you and lift the edge of the omelette with a spatula so that the uncooked egg can run underneath, then tilt the pan away from you and repeat the process.

As soon as the omelette is set but still slightly wet on top, throw in the filling, fold in three and, using the spatula, turn it out onto a plate. That's it! Shouldn't take more than 3 minutes.

{ Egg Whites & Yolks }

MAYONNAISE

This sauce is very easy to make if you follow these instructions carefully. You can halve the quantities if you need less, but it is always more difficult to make when there are only a few yolks. Perfect for an Egg Sandwich (see page 87).

Makes about 1.2 litres (5¼ cups)

6 egg yolks
½ teaspoon salt
1 teaspoon Dijon mustard
500 ml (2¼ cups) **sunflower oil**
500 ml (2¼ cups) **olive oil**
1 teaspoon white wine vinegar or lemon juice
ground black pepper

Beat the egg yolks with the salt, mustard and a pinch of pepper in a bowl until well blended.

Whisking constantly, very gradually add the oils, a drop at a time to start with, then in a continuous stream when the sauce starts to thicken. Keep adding them until all the oil has been used.

If the mix starts to separate, add a teaspoon of cold water and continue.

Add the vinegar or lemon juice at the end, then taste and adjust the seasoning if necessary.

Cover and store in the refrigerator until required.

Do not leave mayonnaise standing at room temperature for too long.

HOLLANDAISE SAUCE

This sauce is best with fish or vegetables, but is also used in the famous Eggs Benedict (see page 33) and Eggs Florentine (see page 33). Like Béarnaise Sauce, it must never be served hot, but kept at a lukewarm temperature.

Makes about 750 ml (3¼ cups)

4 tablespoons white wine vinegar
6 egg yolks
500 g (2½ cups) **butter, melted**
lemon juice, to taste
salt and ground black pepper

Put 4 tablespoons water, the vinegar and a pinch each of salt and pepper into a pan and heat until reduced by two-thirds.

Remove the pan from the heat and whisk in the egg yolks.

Return the pan to low heat and gradually whisk in the melted butter, a little at a time. Add a few drops of cold water if sauce starts to separate. (This also keeps the sauce light.)

Taste and adjust the seasoning, if necessary, and add a few drops of lemon juice. Strain into a bowl and keep warm.

BÉARNAISE SAUCE

This sauce is just wonderful with grilled (broiled) meats of all kinds and is also great with vegetables, especially potatoes.

Makes about 1 litre (4¼ cups)

150 ml (⅔ cup) **white wine vinegar**
150 ml (⅔ cup) **white wine**
3 tablespoons chopped shallots
5 tablespoons chopped fresh tarragon
2½ tablespoons chopped fresh chervil
4–6 black peppercorns
6 egg yolks, beaten
500 g (2½ cups) **butter, melted**
pinch of cayenne pepper
salt

Pour the vinegar and wine into a pan and add the shallots, 4 tablespoons of the tarragon, 2 tablespoons of the chervil, the peppercorns and a pinch of salt.

Set the pan over medium heat and cook until reduced by two-thirds.

Remove from the heat and let cool slightly.

Stir in the egg yolks, return the pan to low heat and carefully whisk in the melted butter, a little at a time. While doing this, occasionally remove the pan from the heat to make sure that the sauce does not get too hot and split.

When the butter has all been incorporated, strain the sauce into a bowl and add the remaining tarragon and chervil.

Season with cayenne pepper and more salt if necessary.

This sauce must never be reheated as it will split, but it can be kept warm in a bain marie (see page 11).

If it starts to separate at any time, you can rescue it by whisking in a teaspoon of cold water or lemon juice.

EGGS
FOR
BREAKFAST

EGGS

Green Fried Eggs
Scrambled Eggs & Vinegar
Scrambled Eggs with Tomato
French Toast
Egg in the Middle
Eggs Benedict
Eggs Florentine
Jane's Eggs
Eggs Baked in Dashi

SCONES
AND
MUFFINS

Date & Walnut Scones
Honey Wholemeal (Whole Wheat) Scones
Chocolate Scones
Cheddar, Leek & Curry Scones
Banana Oat Muffins
Blueberry Muffins
Chocolate Orange Muffins

PANCAKES,
POPOVERS
AND
OATS

Classic Pancakes
Lemon Pancakes
Wholemeal (Whole Wheat) Buttermilk Pancakes
Drop Scones
Popovers
Porridge Oat Pudding

There is no question that breakfast is the most important meal of the day and it is an invariable part of my routine. While I enjoy fruit and cereals, I often opt for an egg-based breakfast, especially when I am particularly tired and need the extra protein boost. Breakfast fans are most particular about this meal above all others and have especially strong opinions about eggs. Whether fried, boiled, poached or scrambled, we know exactly how we like them and nothing can change our minds. In fact, their versatility, familiarity and goodness are the very reasons why we love them. Do try to find time for breakfast, eat slowly and enjoy it.

Our weekend brunch menu at Rose Bakery features the well-loved classics of bacon and eggs, soft-boiled eggs, omelettes and so on *(see page 19)*. However, we like to add some special variations such as Eggs Benedict *(see page 33)*, Scrambled Eggs with Tomato *(see page 29)* and Eggs Baked in Dashi *(see page 34)*. Children, who can sometimes be unenthusiastic about eating breakfast, always enjoy French Toast and Egg in the Middle *(see page 30)*, while family favourites from pancakes *(see pages 42-45)* to scones (biscuits) and muffins *(see pages 36-40)* are a treat for young and old alike.

{ Chocolate Orange Muffins }

{ Green Fried Eggs }

GREEN FRIED EGGS

Serves 1

150–225 g (5–8 ounces) **spinach, coarse
  stalks removed**
2 tablespoons olive oil
2 eggs
salt and ground black pepper
1 tablespoon chopped fresh flat-leaf parsley

Bring a pan of water to the boil, add the spinach and cook for 2 minutes, until wilted.

Drain well and squeeze out the excess moisture, then spread it out on a plate.

Heat the oil in a frying pan or skillet over low to medium heat.

Break the eggs into the pan and cook gently for 1 minute, then sprinkle the parsley over them and season with salt and pepper.

Cover the pan with a lid and cook for about 1 minute more so that the eggs and herbs steam together.

Remove the lid and check that the whites have set.

Lift out the eggs with a rubber spatula, place on top of the spinach and serve. A green, yellow and white story.

SCRAMBLED EGGS & VINEGAR

You can reverse this recipe to make it classic scrambled eggs served with vinegared toast. To make this toast soak sliced bread in a mixture of white wine vinegar, olive oil, salt and pepper and toast in a preheated oven, 220°C/425°F/Gas Mark 7, for a few minutes until lightly golden and crisp.

Serves 1

3 eggs
¾ teaspoon red wine vinegar
50 g (4 tablespoons) **butter**
salt and ground black pepper
warm toast, to serve

Beat the eggs with a large pinch of salt, some pepper and the vinegar in a bowl.

Melt the butter in a pan over low heat. When it has melted add the eggs and scramble until soft and creamy (see page 19).

Tip onto a plate and serve with warm toast.

SCRAMBLED EGGS WITH TOMATO

This has to be my favourite way of cooking eggs for breakfast, but my advice is make it when tomatoes are at their best in summer.

Serves 4

4 tablespoons olive oil
5 tomatoes, peeled, seeded and chopped
2 garlic cloves, mashed
1 heaped teaspoon sugar
50 g (4 tablespoons) **butter**
10 eggs, beaten
4–6 fresh basil leaves, finely shredded
salt and ground black pepper

Heat the oil in a pan, add the tomatoes, garlic and sugar and season with salt and pepper.

Cook over medium heat for 15–20 minutes, until the tomatoes are soft and luscious and all the liquid has evaporated. They should be shiny with olive oil.

Taste and add more sugar or salt, if necessary.

Reduce the heat to low, add the butter and eggs to the pan and stir gently with a wooden spoon until the eggs thicken and come together.

Remove from the heat and stir for a few seconds more until creamy and soft.

Fold in the shredded basil leaves and serve immediately.

There are many variations of scrambled eggs and you can add what you like best. My other favourites include chopped chives or cooked shiitake mushrooms.

FRENCH TOAST

This takes its name from the French dessert *pain perdu*, but is also widely known as eggy bread. It is the simplest way to use up old bread, although you can use fresh. It's also a good way to persuade children who think they don't like eggs to eat them.

Serves 4

3 eggs
175 ml (¾ cup) **milk**
4 slices bread
40 g (3 tablespoons) **butter**
salt

For the topping (optional), to taste

ground cinnamon and sugar
clear honey
icing (confectioners') **sugar**
grated zest of 1 lemon rubbed into sugar
maple syrup
almond butter
yeast extract

Beat the eggs and milk and a pinch of salt in a bowl, then strain into a shallow dish.

Add 1 slice of bread and let soak for about 20 minutes, turning once, as this is best when the bread has soaked up plenty of egg mix. Soak the remaining slices in the same way.

Meanwhile, melt the butter in a large frying pan or skillet.

Add 2 slices of soaked bread and cook over medium heat for about 2 minutes on each side, until golden.

Remove from the pan and cook the remaining slices in the same way.

Serve immediately with your choice of topping.

EGG IN THE MIDDLE

This is an old family favourite and was, apart from pancakes, the only way my children would eat eggs. They called them 'poofle' eggs, although I can't remember why. They are known by many other names, some more logical than others, including knothole eggs, bird's nest, Hollywood eggs and one-eyed Jack.

Serves 2

2 slices bread, preferably wholemeal (whole wheat)
2–3 tablespoons olive oil
2 eggs

First stamp a circle from the centre of each slice of bread with a 5 cm (2 inch) cookie cutter and reserve.

Heat 2 tablespoons of the oil in a frying pan or skillet over medium heat, add the bread and reserved rounds ('hats') and fry until the undersides are lightly golden.

Turn the bread over, adding more oil if necessary.

Carefully break the eggs and ease them into the holes. (I sometimes drain off a little of the white, but this is not a rule.)

Reduce the heat and cook until the whites are set and the yolks are beginning to set, but are still soft.

Using a spatula, transfer the slices of bread and eggs to a plate, with their hats over the yolks, and serve.

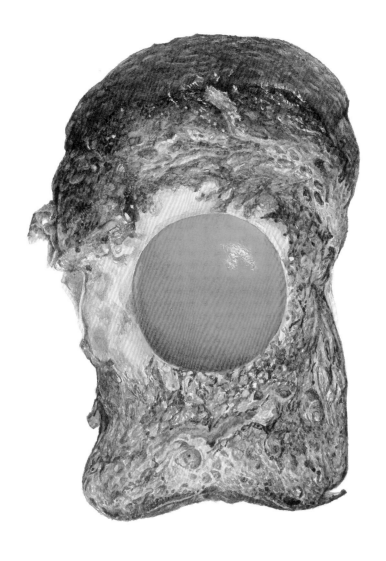

{ Egg in the Middle }

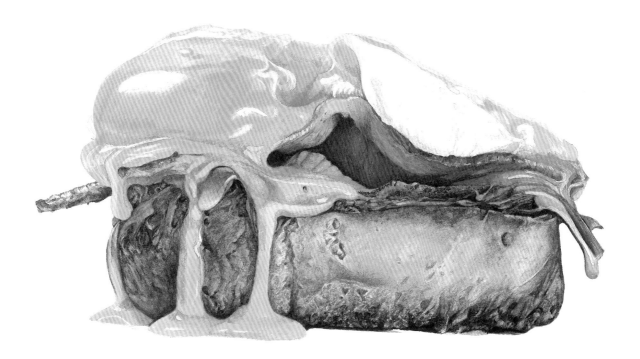

{ Eggs Benedict }

EGGS BENEDICT

I think we kept this off our menu for so long because I felt a little guilty, that we did not make the brioche bread ourselves, but now we do. At Rose Bakery we sometimes break with tradition and serve bacon instead of ham and sometimes we serve it with spinach (see Eggs Florentine) due to customer demand. This works well too.

Serves 3

3 slices brioche
6 slices good-quality ham, preferably carved off the bone or cooked bacon
6 eggs
½ quantity Hollandaise Sauce (see page 21)

Toast both sides of the brioche and put on individual serving plates.

Divide the ham or bacon between the slices of brioche.

Poach the eggs (see page 19), then carefully place on top of the ham.

Spoon over the hollandaise sauce and serve immediately.

EGGS FLORENTINE

This is a variation of Eggs Benedict in which cooked spinach is substituted for the ham.

Serves 4

1 kg (2¼ pounds) **spinach, coarse stalks removed**
25 g (2 tablespoons) **butter or 2 tablespoons olive oil**
4 slices brioche
pinch of freshly grated nutmeg
8 eggs
1 quantity Hollandaise Sauce (see page 21)
salt and ground black pepper

Put the spinach with the water still clinging to the leaves after washing into a pan and add the butter or oil.

Cook over low heat for 5–10 minutes, until wilted.

Meanwhile, toast the bread on both sides and put on individual serving plates.

Add the nutmeg to the spinach and season with salt and pepper.

Strain well and squeeze out the excess liquid.

Divide the spinach among the slices of brioche.

Poach the eggs (see page 19), then carefully place on top of the spinach.

Spoon over the hollandaise sauce and serve immediately.

JANE'S EGGS

One of our chefs told me of her favourite alternative to Eggs Benedict and Eggs Florentine.

She puts a few thin slices of anchovy preserved in oil on top of the poached eggs, adds a few chopped capers to the hollandaise sauce and a sprinkle of chopped fresh flat-leaf parsley on top.

EGGS BAKED IN DASHI

This is our version of *oeufs en cocotte*. Dashi is a Japanese stock made from kombu seaweed and dried fish, and is available as granules and as concentrated liquid (see page 12). I like my baked eggs topped with a sprinkling of crumbled toasted nori seaweed and sesame seeds. This is a good healthy breakfast that is not sweet.

Serves 4

butter or oil, for greasing
175 ml (¾ cup) **hot dashi or vegetable stock** (broth)
8 eggs

Grease 4 small gratin dishes or ovenproof glass ramekins with butter or brush with oil.

Preheat the oven to 180°C/350°F/Gas Mark 4 and put the prepared dishes into it to heat up.

When the oven is hot, remove the dishes, add 3 tablespoons of hot stock to each and return to the oven to heat for a few minutes.

Remove from the oven and add 2 eggs to each dish.

Put the dishes into a roasting pan, pour in warm water to come about a third of the way up their sides, cover with foil and bake for about 15 minutes, until the eggs are just set.

Remove from the oven and serve immediately.

Variations of this recipe include eggs baked with the following combinations:

– Cream and chives
– Chopped anchovies topped with chopped fresh flat-leaf parsley
– Diced ham topped with grated cheese
– Sautéed mushrooms and cream
– Cooked spinach with cream and grated Parmesan cheese
– Petits pois and shredded lettuce
– Tomato sauce and tarragon

If you are using cream, always make sure that it is hot when you add the eggs, as this will help them to cook evenly.

Use 1–2 tablespoons cream per dish, and we usually serve 2 eggs per portion.

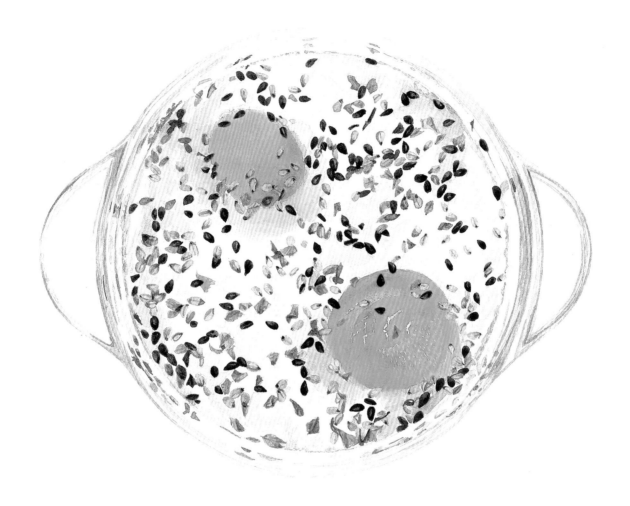

{ Eggs Baked in Dashi }

Although scones, known as biscuits in the US, are often thought of as teatime treats, they can be eaten at any time of the day and are especially nice for breakfast with butter and jam. Breakfast scones made with a dough containing eggs are usually denser and more substantial than light tea scones, so it is important to handle the dough as little as possible to avoid it becoming heavy. Lightly beaten egg on its own, or mixed with a little water, can be brushed over the top of the scones before baking to give them an attractive glaze.

DATE & WALNUT SCONES

Makes 12

120 g (1 cup) **self-raising flour, plus extra for dusting**
175 g (1½ cups) **wholemeal** (whole wheat) **flour**
1 heaped teaspoon bicarbonate of soda (baking soda)
pinch salt
½ teaspoon mixed (apple pie) **spice**
1 tablespoon brown sugar
7 pitted dates
100 g (scant 1 cup) **walnuts**
100 g (scant ½ cup) **butter**
1 egg
200 ml (scant 1 cup) **buttermilk**
beaten egg, to glaze (optional)

Preheat the oven to 200°C/400°F/Gas Mark 6 and line a baking sheet with baking parchment.

Put both types of flour, the bicarbonate of soda, salt, spice, sugar, dates and walnuts in a food processor and process until the mixture resembles fresh breadcrumbs. Alternatively, finely chop the dates and walnuts and mix in a bowl with both types of flour, the bicarbonate of soda, salt, spice and sugar.

Add the butter and rub in with your fingertips until the mixture resembles fresh breadcrumbs. Make a well in the middle. Lightly beat the egg with the buttermilk in another bowl and pour into the well.

Using a fork, stir to mix, finishing by hand to bring the dough together. Do not overwork the dough – it should just come together softly but firmly.

Roll or pat out the dough on a lightly floured surface to about 3 cm (1¼ inches) thick.

Carefully stamp out 5 cm (2 inch) rounds and put them on the prepared baking sheet. Brush with beaten egg if you like. Bake for about 20 minutes, until lightly golden and firm to the touch.

{ Date & Walnut Scones }

HONEY WHOLEMEAL (WHOLE WHEAT) SCONES

Makes 12

225 g (2 cups) **self-raising flour, plus extra for dusting**
120 g (1 cup) **wholemeal** (whole wheat) **flour mixed with 1 tablespoon baking powder**
50 g (½ cup) **rolled oats**
½ teaspoon salt
60 g (4½ tablespoons) **butter**
175 g (¾ cup) **well-flavoured honey such as heather**
1 egg
175 ml (¾ cup) **milk**
lightly beaten egg, to glaze (optional)

Preheat the oven to 200°C/400°F/Gas Mark 6 and line a baking sheet with baking parchment.

Put both types of flour, baking powder, the oats and salt into a bowl.

Add the butter and rub in with your fingertips until the mixture resembles breadcrumbs.

Make a well in the middle. Lightly beat the egg with the milk in another bowl and pour into the well.

Using a fork, stir to mix, finishing by hand to bring the dough together. Do not overwork this dough – it should be soft but firm and not sticky or dry. Add a little more flour if is sticky, or a little more milk if it is dry.

Roll or pat out the dough on a lightly floured surface to about 3 cm (1¼ inches) thick.

Carefully stamp out 5 cm (2 inch) rounds and put them on the prepared baking sheet.

Brush with beaten egg if you like.

Bake for about 20 minutes, until golden and firm to the touch.

Serve warm or cold with butter and jam.

CHOCOLATE SCONES

I know this might seem a strange idea, but somehow these scones are very satisfying. It's like chocolate cereals – if you like chocolate for breakfast, these are for you.

Makes 18

250 ml (1 cup) **milk or single** (light) **cream**
2 eggs
1 teaspoon vanilla extract
550 g (5 cups) **plain** (all-purpose)**, plus extra for dusting**
50 g (½ cup) **unsweetened cocoa powder**
150 g (¾ cup) **caster** (superfine) **sugar**
2 tablespoons baking powder
½ teaspoon salt
140 g (generous ½ cup) **butter**
350–400 g (2–2⅓ cups) **chocolate chips**
lightly beaten egg, to glaze (optional)

Preheat the oven to 200°C/400°F/Gas Mark 6 and line a baking sheet with baking parchment.

Lightly beat together the milk or cream, eggs and vanilla in a bowl.

Put the flour, cocoa powder, sugar, baking powder and salt into another bowl.

Add the butter and rub in with your fingertips until the mixture resembles fresh breadcrumbs.

Stir in the chocolate chips, make a well in the middle and pour in the milk mixture.

Using a fork, stir to mix, finishing by hand to bring the dough together. Do not overwork the dough – it should just come together softly but firmly.

Roll or pat out the dough on a lightly floured surface to about 3 cm (1¼ inches) thick.

Carefully stamp out 5 cm (2 inch) rounds and put them on the prepared baking sheet.

Brush with beaten egg if you like.

Bake for 15–20 minutes, until firm to the touch.

CHEDDAR, LEEK & CURRY SCONES

These scones are great simply buttered and served on their own, but they also go well with scrambled eggs, and are a delicious accompaniment to soups at lunchtime.

Makes 18

500 g (4½ cups) **self-raising flour,**
  plus extra for dusting
4 tablespoons caster (superfine) **sugar**
2 teaspoons curry powder
½ teaspoon salt
100 g (scant ½ cup) **butter**
60 g (generous ½ cup) **grated Cheddar cheese**
2 eggs
about 120 ml (½ cup) **sour cream**
lightly beaten egg, to glaze

For the leeks

40 g (3 tablespoons) **butter**
1 tablespoon olive oil
250 g (9 ounces) **leeks, thinly sliced**
1 teaspoon sugar
salt and ground black pepper

Preheat the oven to 200°C/400°F/Gas Mark 6 and line a baking sheet with baking parchment.

First, prepare the leeks. Melt the butter with the oil in a pan, add the leeks and cook over low heat, stirring occasionally, for 10–15 minutes, until very soft.

Stir in the sugar, season with salt and pepper and leave to cool, then chill in the refrigerator.

Meanwhile, put the flour, sugar, curry powder and salt into a bowl, add the butter and rub in with your fingertips until the mixture resembles fresh breadcrumbs.

Stir in the cheese and make a well in the middle.

Lightly beat the eggs with 3 tablespoons of the sour cream in a bowl, stir in the leek mixture, and pour into the well.

Using a fork, stir to mix, finishing by hand to bring the dough together, adding the remaining cream if necessary. Do not overwork the dough – it should just come together softly but firmly.

Roll or pat out the dough on a lightly floured surface to about 3 cm (1¼ inches) thick.

Carefully stamp out 4–5 cm (1½–2 inch) rounds and put them on the prepared baking sheet.

Brush with beaten egg to glaze.

Bake for about 20 minutes, until golden.

BANANA OAT MUFFINS

Makes about 10

butter, for greasing
80 g (¾ cup) **wholemeal** (whole wheat) **flour**
280 g (2⅓ cups) **plain** (all-purpose) **flour**
50 g (½ cup) **rolled oats, plus extra to decorate**
120 g (½ cup) **brown sugar**
½ teaspoon bicarbonate of soda (baking soda)
2 teaspoons baking powder
½ teaspoon salt
6 bananas
grated zest of 2 lemons
½ teaspoon vanilla extract
3 eggs
200 ml (scant 1 cup) **milk or buttermilk**
120 g (½ cup) **butter, melted**
5–6 teaspoons mixed ground cinnamon
  and sugar

Preheat the oven to 200°C/400°F/Gas Mark 6.

Grease and line a 10 cup muffin pan with butter and baking parchment.

Mix together both types of flour, the oats, sugar, bicarbonate of soda, baking powder and salt in a bowl.

Mash 2 bananas and slice the remainder.

Beat together the mashed banana, lemon zest, vanilla, eggs, milk and melted butter in another bowl.

Stir the sliced bananas into the dry ingredients, then gently fold in the mashed banana mixture. Don't overmix, as this will make the muffins heavy and dense.

Fill the prepared muffin cups to about three-quarters full and top with a sprinkling of rolled oats and cinnamon and sugar.

Bake for about 25 minutes.

BLUEBERRY MUFFINS

These muffins were inspired by a recipe from the Tassajara Zen Mountain Center, California, renowned for its vegetarian cuisine and artisan baking. They are among the best muffins I have eaten as they are wholesome and not sweet. We also use this recipe as a base for other muffins, so when blueberries are not in season we add raspberries, finely diced apples or diced fresh apricots. So do use your favourite ingredients instead of blueberries if you wish.

Makes about 10

butter, for greasing
150 g (1¼ cups) wholemeal (whole wheat) flour
280 g (2⅓ cups) plain (all-purpose) flour
120 g (½ cup) brown sugar
½ teaspoon bicarbonate of soda (baking soda)
2 teaspoons baking powder
½ teaspoon salt
2 bananas, mashed
grated zest of 2 lemons
½ teaspoon vanilla extract
3 eggs
200 ml (scant 1 cup) milk or buttermilk
120 g (½ cup) butter, melted
150 g (1 cup) blueberries, plus extra for decoration
5–6 teaspoons mixed ground cinnamon and sugar

Preheat the oven to 200°C/400°F/Gas Mark 6.

Grease and line a 10 cup muffin pan with butter and baking parchment.

Mix together both types of flour, the sugar, bicarbonate of soda, baking powder and salt in a bowl.

Beat together the mashed banana, lemon zest, vanilla, eggs, milk and melted butter in another bowl.

Stir the blueberries into the dry ingredients, then gently fold in the banana mixture. Don't overmix, as this will make the muffins heavy and dense.

Fill the prepared muffin cups to about three-quarters full and top with a few extra blueberries and a sprinkling of cinnamon and sugar.

Bake for about 25 minutes.

CHOCOLATE ORANGE MUFFINS

Makes 6–8

butter, for greasing
225 g (2 cups) plain flour
100 g (½ cup) caster (superfine) sugar
40 g (⅓ cup) unsweetened cocoa powder
1½ teaspoons baking powder
½ teaspoon salt
100 g (generous ½ cup) chocolate chips
2 eggs
175 ml (¾ cup) milk
1 teaspoon vanilla extract
grated zest of 2 oranges
120 ml (½ cup) sour cream
100 g (7 tablespoons) butter, melted
melted chocolate and glacé (candied) orange, to decorate (optional)

Preheat oven to 200°C/400°F/Gas Mark 6.

Grease and line a 6–8 cup muffin pan with butter and baking parchment.

Sift together the flour, sugar, cocoa powder, baking powder and salt into a bowl and stir in the chocolate chips.

Beat together the eggs, milk, vanilla, orange zest, sour cream and melted butter in another bowl, then carefully fold into the dry ingredients without overmixing until the mixture just comes together.

Fill the prepared muffin cups to about three-quarters full and bake for about 20 minutes.

We sometimes drizzle melted chocolate on top when the muffins have cooled and a slice of glacé orange if available.

{ Blueberry Muffins }

Pancakes, Popovers and Oats

Pancakes are a particularly popular choice on our menu at weekends, when customers enjoy them as part of a relaxing and leisurely brunch. Of course, they're just as much of a delicious treat as breakfast for early birds. Classic pancakes feature frequently on our menus and we also offer an assortment of other pancakes from time to time.

Accompaniments vary throughout the year depending on the fruit of the season. They include sliced bananas, fresh and cooked blueberries, raspberries, apple compote and maple or yacón syrup (*see page* 13).

In addition to pancakes, we sometimes make popovers (a sweet Yorkshire pudding) and occasionally a porridge oat pudding, which is perfect for cold mornings in the winter.

CLASSIC PANCAKES

Serves 4–6

2 eggs
220 ml (scant 1 cup) **milk**
60 g (4½ tablespoons) **butter, melted, plus extra for greasing**
175 g (1¼ cups) **self-raising or plain** (all-purpose) **flour**
½ teaspoon salt
4 teaspoons baking powder, if using plain (all-purpose) **flour**
1 teaspoon caster (superfine) **sugar**

Whisk together the eggs, milk and melted butter in a bowl.

Sift the flour, salt, baking powder (if using) and sugar into another bowl.

Pour the egg mixture into the dry ingredients and gently fold it in. Take care not to overmix; in fact there should still be some small bits of dry flour in the mix... just a little.

Grease a frying pan or skillet with a little butter and set over medium-high heat.

When the pan is hot, drop about 3 tablespoons for each pancake into the pan, without over-crowding it, and cook until bubbles start to appear on the surface.

Turn the pancakes over and cook for another 30 seconds, until golden.

Transfer to a warm dish and keep warm while you cook the remaining pancakes.

Serve immediately with maple syrup and blueberries or your accompaniments of choice.

{ Classic Pancakes }

LEMON PANCAKES

What I love about these pancakes – apart from their lovely lemony flavour – is that they don't contain baking powder, which sometimes leaves a slightly metallic taste in the mouth. However, this means that special care should be taken with the egg whites, whisking them well and folding in gently without knocking the air out.

Makes about 10

3 eggs, separated
2 tablespoons caster (superfine) **sugar**
60 g (4½ tablespoons) **butter, melted, plus**
  extra for greasing
175 g (¾ cup) **ricotta cheese**
40 g (⅓ cup) **plain** (all-purpose) **flour**
grated zest of 2 lemons
1 teaspoon lemon juice
salt

Mix together the egg yolks, sugar, melted butter, ricotta and a pinch of salt in a bowl.

Fold in the flour, lemon zest and juice.

Whisk the egg whites in a grease-free bowl until quite firm, then carefully fold into the egg yolk mixture.

Grease a frying pan or skillet with a little butter and set over medium-high heat.

When the pan is hot, drop about 3 tablespoons for each pancake into the pan, without overcrowding it, and cook until bubbles start to appear on the surface.

Turn the pancakes over and cook for another 30 seconds, until golden.

Transfer to a warm dish and keep warm while you cook the remaining pancakes.

These pancakes go beautifully with crushed raspberries, or spiced apple or pear compote.

WHOLEMEAL (WHOLE WHEAT) BUTTERMILK PANCAKES

These have to be my favourite pancakes because of the wholegrains and also because you can choose lots of combinations to suit your taste. For instance, you can use other mixtures of flours, such as wholemeal (whole wheat), spelt and oat, or plain (all-purpose), rye and buckwheat. Different flours will change the flavour and some might make the pancakes a little denser.

Makes about 8 pancakes

300 ml (1¼ cups) **buttermilk**
1 egg
50 g (4 tablespoons) **butter, melted, plus**
  extra for greasing
50 g (½ cup) **wholemeal** (whole wheat) **flour**
4 tablespoons plain (all-purpose) **flour**
4 tablespoons rye flour
½ teaspoon salt
1 teaspoon brown sugar
1 rounded teaspoon bicarbonate of soda
  (baking soda)

Whisk together the buttermilk, egg and melted butter in a bowl.

Mix together all the dry ingredients in another bowl, then gently fold in the buttermilk mixture. Do not overmix.

Grease a frying pan or skillet with a little butter and set over medium-high heat.

When the pan is hot, drop about 3 tablespoons for each pancake into the pan, without overcrowding it, and cook until bubbles start to appear on the surface.

Turn the pancakes over and cook for another 30 seconds, until golden.

Transfer to a warm dish and keep warm while you cook the remaining pancakes.

You can serve these with maple syrup, toasted seeds or nuts, a sprinkling of muesli or granola, or fruit.

DROP SCONES

Also called Scottish pancakes, these are not really scones (biscuits) at all. They are cooked on a griddle (grill pan) or in a frying pan or skillet just like pancakes.

Makes 12–16

250 g (2¼ cups) **wholemeal** (whole wheat)
  flour mixed with 1½ teaspoons baking powder
¾ tablespoon caster (superfine) **sugar**
2 eggs, lightly beaten
50 g (4 tablespoons) **butter, melted, plus extra**
  for greasing
about 250 ml (1 cup) **milk**
salt
demerara (turbinado) **sugar, honey or jam,**
  to serve

Mix the flour, sugar and a pinch of salt in a bowl.

Make a well in the middle and add the beaten eggs, melted butter and a little of the milk.

Stir with a fork to incorporate all the dry ingredients, adding more milk until you have a thick batter.

Grease a frying pan or skillet with a little butter and set over medium–high heat.

When the pan is hot, drop spoonfuls of the batter into the pan, without overcrowding it, and cook until bubbles start to appear on the surface.

Turn the pancakes over and cook for 1 minute more, until golden.

Transfer to a warm dish and keep warm while you cook the remaining pancakes.

Serve immediately with a sprinkling of sugar or with honey or jam.

{ Popovers }

POPOVERS

You don't have to wait for a roast dinner to enjoy traditional English Yorkshire puddings when you can eat this sugar-topped version for breakfast. You can also serve these with maple syrup, fruit jam or warm apple compote. Muffin pans are ideal for baking them as they are deeper than they are wide.

Makes about 12

6 eggs
350 ml (1½ cups) **milk**
175 g (1½ cups) **plain** (all-purpose) **flour**
½ teaspoon salt
250 g (generous 1 cup) **butter**
icing (confectioners') **sugar and lemon juice, to serve**

Preheat the oven to a hot 220°C/425°F/Gas Mark 7.

Beat the eggs with the milk in a bowl, add the flour and salt all at once and fold in gently. Be careful not to overmix. The batter will remain slightly lumpy.

Melt the butter in a pan over low heat and pour about 2 tablespoons into each of 12 muffin cups.

Pour the batter over the butter and immediately put into the oven.

Bake for about 20 minutes, or until the popovers are golden brown and well puffed up.

Sprinkle them with icing sugar and a little lemon juice and serve immediately.

PORRIDGE OAT PUDDING

I have oat porridge nearly every morning as I think it's one of the best ways to start the day. This pudding is a rather more substantial affair but is a delicious way to eat oats.

Serves 4

20 g (3 tablespoons) **butter, plus extra for greasing**
250 ml (1 cup) **milk or soy milk**
80 g (¾ cup) **rolled oats**
50 ml (¼ cup) **double** (heavy) **cream, plus extra for serving**
50 g (¼ cup) **brown sugar**
½ teaspoon ground cinnamon
3 eggs, separated
salt
chopped toasted walnuts, to decorate

Preheat oven to 180°C/350°F/Gas Mark 4.

Generously grease 4 ramekins with butter.

Pour the milk into a pan, add the butter and bring just to simmering point over medium-low heat.

Reduce the heat down, stir in the porridge oats and cook, stirring constantly, until smooth and thick.

Remove the pan from the heat and stir in the cream, sugar, cinnamon and a pinch of salt.

Beat the egg yolks in a bowl and stir in.

Whisk the whites in a grease-free bowl until stiff and gently fold into the mixture. Don't overmix.

Divide the mixture among the ramekins and bake for 40 minutes, until almost set.

Remove from the oven, sprinkle with toasted nuts and serve immediately with more cream.

This is also delicious with apple compote.

EGGS
FOR
LUNCH

SOUPS

Egg Soup
Chicken Soup with Passatelli
Chicken Soup & Kneidlach
Italian Egg Soup
Tomato, Porcini (Cep) & Egg Soup
Poached Eggs in Tomato & Fennel Broth
Tofu Hot Pot

GRATINS

Courgette (Zucchini) & Tomato Gratin
Courgette (Zucchini) & Aubergine (Eggplant) Gratin
Leek, Tomato & Mustard Gratin

TARTS

Basic Pastry Dough
Green Tarts
Leek & Mustard Tarts
Curried Cauliflower Tarts

MAIN COURSES

Tarragon Chicken
Meatballs
Tofu Balls
Lentil & Whole Grain Fritters
Buckwheat Crêpes
Three-Coloured Frittata
Lacy Eggs over Vegetables
Rose Bakery Ratatouille
Mashed Potatoes, Eggs & Parmesan
Spinach & Ricotta Gnocchi

SAVOURY CUSTARDS

Traditional Chawanmushi
My Chawanmushi with Spring Vegetables
My Chawanmushi with Seafood

SALADS

Our Salad Niçoise
Egg & Cress Salad
Egg Salad with Arame & Rice
Cauliflower & Egg Curry Salad
Leek Vinaigrette with Eggs & Herbs

LIGHT LUNCHES

Egg Sandwich
Club Sandwich
Omelette Sandwich
Curried Egg Sandwich
Scotch Eggs

Lunch is for lucky people with time. Behind the scenes in restaurants and cafés we are always too busy. That's why, whenever I have a day off, it is such a treat just to sit and eat a leisurely lunch at home or in a restaurant. I have often been scolded for not taking the time to eat lunch and it is important to do so. Eggs are a great choice for lunch dishes, as most people keep them in stock in the refrigerator, they are tremendously versatile and very quick and easy to prepare and cook.

I love to eat soups all year round, except when the weather is very hot, and these are some of my favourite recipes. They do take a little longer to prepare but are well worth it. I do love eating out of bowls, so also really enjoy chawanmushis – steamed savoury custards – meatballs, gratins and salads. There is just something comforting about bowls and whether I eat with chopsticks or a fork I have the same good feeling. Perhaps this also stems from my love of both Japanese and Italian food. Vegetable tarts with an egg and cream filling require a little more time and effort but are truly rewarding and a great choice for weekend lunches and picnics. Like everyone else, I am often so pressed for time that only a sandwich will do – but not just any sandwich. My favourite has to be egg and cress.

{ Lacy Eggs over Vegetables }

Soups

I love soups and could easily live on them alone. We always have at least one soup on the menu and they are always popular. There are so many different varieties and combinations but these are some of my favourites. The inclusion of eggs makes them a complete meal – delicious and nourishing.

EGG SOUP

Serves 4

1 litre (4¼ cups) **dashi (see page 12)
  or vegetable stock**
1 teaspoon soy sauce
1 teaspoon sugar
1 teaspoon arrowroot or cornflour (cornstarch)
handful of sprouted mung beans
2–3 spring onions (scallions)**, chopped**
**handful soft salad leaves, such as lamb's
  lettuce** (corn salad)**, plus extra to garnish**
4 eggs, beaten

Pour the stock into a pan and bring to a boil, then add the soy sauce and sugar.

Mix the arrowroot or cornflour with 1 teaspoon water to a smooth paste in a small bowl and add to the soup, stirring well.

Reduce the heat and simmer for a few minutes, until the soup has thickened slightly. Stir briskly to create a whirlpool, then add the sprouted beans, spring onions and lamb's lettuce, followed immediately by the eggs.

Cook gently until the eggs have set at the top. Serve immediately, garnished with extra shredded lamb's lettuce leaves.

CHICKEN SOUP WITH PASSATELLI

The first time I ever ate this soup was at least 20 years ago in a small back-street restaurant in Bologna in northern Italy. I had no idea what it was, but everyone was eating it so I just pointed and asked for it too. When this wonderful broth arrived with the delicious soft noodles I was completely seduced – total heaven. It was several years later that I obtained a good recipe and several more before I finally got a ricer. To make this dish you will need a good ricer with holes at least 5 mm (¼ inch) in diameter or a colander with 5 mm (¼ inch) holes.

Serves 4

100 g (1¾ cups) **fine fresh breadcrumbs**
100 g (generous 1 cup) **finely grated
  Parmesan cheese**
grated zest of 1 lemon
¼ teaspoon grated nutmeg
2–3 eggs, beaten
1 litre (4¼ cups) **good quality chicken broth
  or stock**
salt and ground black pepper

Combine the breadcrumbs, Parmesan, lemon zest and nutmeg in a bowl, add most of the beaten egg and mix well to a fairly soft dough, adding more beaten egg if the mixture is too dry. (If it is too soft, add more breadcrumbs.)

Cover with clingfilm (plastic wrap) and let rest in a cool place, but not the refrigerator, for about 30 minutes.

Spread out a sheet of greaseproof (wax) paper and press the dough through a ricer, cutting off 3–4 cm (1¼–1½ inch) long noodles. Separate them and let dry for about 1 hour. Bring the broth or stock to a simmer in a large pan, add the passatelli and cook for 1–2 minutes. Serve immediately.

You can add finely chopped parsley to the passatelli mixture or even a little minced (ground) mortadella.

CHICKEN SOUP & KNEIDLACH

While we are on the subject of chicken soup, I have to share my mother's matzo meal dumplings (kneidlach) recipe. It happens to be the best I have ever eaten. You will need a wonderful chicken broth or stock, that is either clear or contains finely diced vegetables. A good-quality vegetable broth also works well.

Serves 4

2 large (US extra large) **eggs, separated**
2 tablespoons vegetable oil or melted chicken fat
50 g (scant ½ cup) **matzo meal**
pinch of ground cinnamon (optional)
1 litre (4¼ cups) **good-quality chicken or vegetable broth or stock**
chopped fresh flat-leaf parsley or chives, to garnish
salt and ground black pepper

Beat the egg whites with a pinch of salt in a grease-free bowl until quite stiff but not dry.

Fold in the egg yolks and the oil or melted fat. Carefully fold in the matzo meal until thoroughly combined and season with salt, pepper and the cinnamon. The mixture should be soft and not dry. Add more matzo meal if too soft. Do not overwork the mixture.

Wrap in clingfilm (plastic wrap) and chill in the refrigerator for about 30 minutes.

Remove the dumpling mixture from the refrigerator and roll into 2–3 cm (¾–1¼ inch) balls.

Dampening your hands slightly will make this easier.

Bring a pan of lightly salted water to a boil, then reduce the heat to a simmer.

Drop the balls into the water and simmer for 15 minutes, until they float to the surface. Remove with a slotted spoon and drain.

When ready to serve, heat the broth or stock in a large pan until it is simmering, drop in the balls and heat through for 5–10 minutes.

Serve in bowls garnished with chopped parsley or chives.

My mother sometimes adds a handful of ground almonds to the dumpling mixture. This makes them denser but also delicious.

ITALIAN EGG SOUP

Known as *stracciatella* in Italy, this is a restorative soup that I have always loved. Some people like to add spinach to this soup, but you could add any other salad leaf too, such as rocket (arugula) or lamb's lettuce (corn salad). There are, as always with Italian dishes, many versions but I think the simplest is the best.

Serves 4

1.2 litres (5 cups) **chicken or vegetable broth or stock**
2 eggs, beaten
25 g (¼ cup) **ground almonds or 40 g** (¼ cup) **semolina**
25 g (⅓ cup) **grated Parmesan cheese, plus extra to garnish (optional)**
pinch of grated nutmeg
3 tablespoons chopped fresh flat-leaf parsley, plus extra to garnish (optional)
salt and ground black pepper

Reserve 2 tablespoons of the broth or stock, pour the remainder into a pan and bring to a boil. Reduce the heat to a simmer.

Add the reserved stock to the beaten eggs and mix in the ground almonds or semolina, Parmesan and nutmeg.

Add the parsley to the pan, then immediately pour in the egg mixture. Swirl this around for a few seconds, remove from the heat and serve, garnished with extra Parmesan or chopped parsley.

Some people add some pralines, almonds or other toasted nuts as well on top. But I prefer the simple version.

TOMATO, PORCINI (CEP) & EGG SOUP

This is a broth with lots of interest, rather like
a thin minestrone.

Serves 4

25 g (½ cup) **dried porcini** (dried ceps)
4 tablespoons virgin olive oil
2 onions, finely diced
1 celery stalk, finely diced
pinch of sugar
3 eggs beaten
1 litre (4¼ cups) **chicken or vegetable broth**
  or stock
4 ripe tomatoes, peeled, seeded and chopped
handful fresh basil leaves, torn
salt and ground black pepper

Put the dried mushrooms into a heatproof bowl,
add 250 ml (1 cup) hot water and let soak.

Heat half the olive oil in a pan, add the onions
and celery and cook over medium heat, stirring
occasionally, for 10 minutes, until the onions have
softened. Add the sugar and season with salt.

Meanwhile, heat a little of the remaining olive oil
in a frying pan or skillet. Pour in a small quantity of
the beaten egg and cook until just set, then remove
with a spatula.

Continue making more very thin omelettes in this
way, adding more oil as necessary, until all the
beaten egg has been used.

When these omelettes are cool, roll them up and
shred them into 1 cm (¼ inch) thick strips to make
egg 'noodles'. Set aside.

Add the tomatoes to the vegetables in the pan and
cook for 5 minutes, until softened, then pour in the
broth or stock and add the mushrooms with their
soaking liquid. Simmer for 20 minutes.

Taste and adjust the seasoning, adding salt, sugar
and/or pepper to taste.

Add the basil leaves, ladle into soup bowls, top with
a handful of egg noodles and serve immediately.

{ Tomato, Porcini (Cep) & Egg Soup }

POACHED EGGS IN TOMATO & FENNEL BROTH

The generous quantity of vegetables in this soup makes it more like a stew.

Serves 4

3 tablespoons extra-virgin olive oil
1 onion
pinch of sugar
pinch of chilli flakes
2 garlic cloves, mashed
4 ripe tomatoes, peeled, seeded and chopped or 400 g (7 ounces) **canned tomatoes, drained**
1.5 litres (6¼ cups) **vegetable stock or water**
1 fennel bulb, thinly sliced
salt and ground black pepper

Heat the olive oil in a large pan, add the onion, sugar, chilli and a pinch of salt and cook over low heat, stirring occasionally, for 5–8 minutes, until softened but not brown.

Add the garlic and tomatoes and cook gently for another 5 minutes, until the tomatoes have lost most of their liquid.

Pour in the stock or water and simmer for 10 minutes, then add the fennel and continue cooking for an additional 10 minutes, until it is tender and the stock has reduced slightly.

Taste and adjust the seasoning, adding salt, pepper or sugar if necessary.

With the stock still simmering, ease in the eggs, one at a time if you like, and poach them carefully (see page 19).

Lift out the eggs with a slotted spoon and put them in 4 individual bowls, ladle the stock and vegetables over the top and serve immediately.

TOFU HOT POT

This great restorative one-pot dish is a good way to use up extra vegetables.

Serves 4

1 litre (4¼ cups) **vegetable or chicken stock**
1 onion, cut into bite-size pieces
1 leek, cut into bite-size pieces
2 celery stalks, cut into bite-size pieces
1 carrot, cut into bite-size pieces
½ head spring cabbage, cut into bite-size pieces
4 baby turnips, cut into bite-size pieces
300 g (11 ounces) **firm tofu, cut into large bite-size pieces**
dash of shoyu (see page 13)
2 tablespoons chopped fresh chives
1 tablespoons olive oil (optional)
25 g (2 tablespoons) **butter (optional)**
4 eggs
salt and ground black pepper
hot chilli sauce or Dijon mustard, to serve

Pour the stock into a pan and bring to a simmer.

Add the onion, leek, celery and carrot and simmer for about 5 minutes.

Add the cabbage and turnips and cook for an additional 5–10 minutes, until just tender but not overcooked, then add the tofu and warm through.

Season to taste with shoyu and salt and pepper, if necessary, and add the chives.

The eggs may be fried in olive oil and butter or added to the pan and poached (see page 19).

Transfer the eggs to 4 individual bowls, ladle in the stew and serve immediately with a hot chilli sauce, Japanese chilli powder or Dijon mustard.

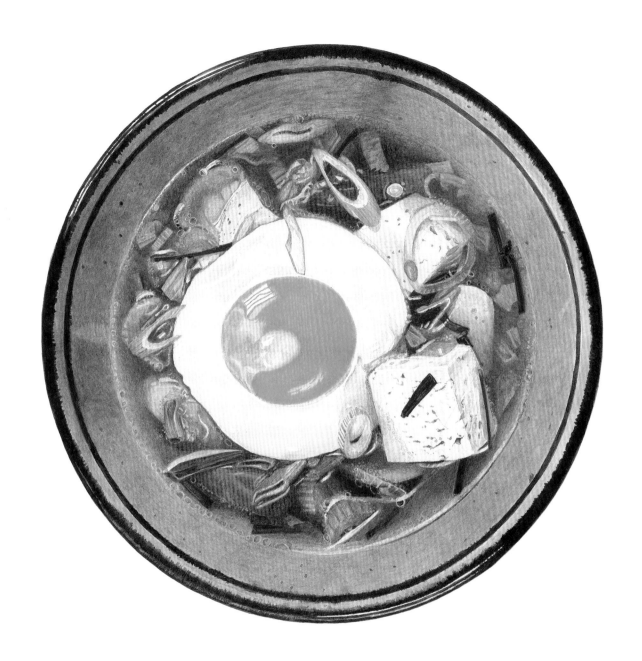

{ Tofu Hot Pot }

Gratins

With such a huge choice of vegetables, fish and meat it is possible to make hundreds of different gratins. Some are baked with cream, others with béchamel sauce and still more with stock or an egg mixture. The recipes here use eggs as the binder for these vegetables, but two also include bread to give more substance, while the other is lighter. All three are delicious.

COURGETTE (ZUCCHINI) & TOMATO GRATIN

You will need 4 pretty cups or heatproof bowls and a steamer or a large casserole (dutch oven) or pan with a lid.

Serves 4–6

butter, for greasing
2 garlic cloves, mashed
7 courgettes (zucchini)**, thinly sliced**
6 ripe tomatoes, thinly sliced
olive oil, for drizzling
5 eggs
5 tablespoons double (heavy) **cream**
½ teaspoon curry powder
pinch of ground cumin
pinch of grated nutmeg
pinch of ground cinnamon
pinch of sugar
salt and ground black pepper

Preheat the oven to 200°C/400°F/Gas Mark 6.

Grease an ovenproof dish with butter and rub with a little of the garlic. Alternate the courgette and tomato slices in concentric circles in the prepared dish, drizzle with olive oil and bake for about 30 minutes, until the vegetables are soft.

Remove the dish from the oven and reduce the oven temperature to 190°C/375°F/Gas Mark 5.

If a lot of liquid has been released by the vegetables, carefully drain it off.

Beat the eggs with the cream, spices and remaining garlic in a bowl and season to taste with salt and pepper.

Pour the mixture over the vegetables, return the dish to the oven and bake for about 30 minutes, until golden.

Remove the dish from the oven and let stand until the gratin is warm rather than hot, then serve.

COURGETTE (ZUCCHINI) & AUBERGINE (EGGPLANT) GRATIN

You will need 4 pretty cups or heatproof bowls and a steamer or a large casserole (dutch oven) or pan with a lid.

Serves 4–6

butter, for greasing
2 tablespoons olive oil, plus extra for drizzling
5 courgettes (zucchini), thinly sliced
3 aubergines (eggplants), cut into 5 mm
   (¼ inch) slices
4 slices stale bread, crusts removed
2 eggs, lightly beaten
100 g (generous 1 cup) grated Parmesan cheese
3–4 tablespoons chopped fresh flat-leaf parsley
2 garlic cloves, mashed
salt and ground black pepper

Preheat the oven to 200°C/400°F/Gas Mark 6.

Grease an ovenproof dish with butter. Heat the oil in a frying pan or skillet, add the courgettes, season with salt and cook over low heat, turning occasionally, for a few minutes, until just beginning to soften, then remove from the heat.

Put the aubergine slices in a roasting pan, drizzle generously with olive oil, season with salt and pepper and roast for 15–20 minutes, until soft.

Meanwhile, tear the bread into pieces, put it into a bowl, add 4 tablespoons water and let soak until soft.

Drain and squeeze out the excess water, then mix the bread with the eggs, Parmesan, parsley and garlic to make a soft, paste-like consistency. Season to taste with salt and pepper.

Remove the aubergines from the oven but do not switch it off. Combine the egg mixture with the courgettes and aubergines in a bowl, spoon the mixture into the prepared dish and smooth the surface. Alternatively, you can make layers of the vegetables and egg mixture.

Drizzle some olive oil on top and bake for about 30 minutes, until lightly golden.

Remove the dish from the oven and let stand until the gratin is warm rather than hot, then serve.

LEEK, TOMATO & MUSTARD GRATIN

You will need 4 pretty cups or heatproof bowls and a steamer or a large casserole (dutch oven) or pan with a lid.

Serves 6

butter, for greasing
1 garlic clove, halved
6 tablespoons olive oil
6 leeks, thinly sliced
pinch of sugar
5 ripe tomatoes, cored and thinly sliced
120 g (2 cups) fine fresh breadcrumbs
3–4 tablespoons chopped fresh flat-leaf parsley
3 eggs
600 ml (2½ cups) double (heavy) cream
2 tablespoons Dijon mustard
pinch of grated nutmeg
salt and ground black pepper

Preheat the oven to 180°C/350°F/Gas Mark 4.

Grease an ovenproof dish with butter and rub with the garlic. Heat 2 tablespoons of the olive oil in a frying pan or skillet, add the leeks and cook over low heat, stirring occasionally, for 8–10 minutes, until softened and most of the liquid has evaporated.

Remove from the heat and season to taste with the sugar, salt and pepper.

Spoon the leeks into the prepared dish and top with the sliced tomatoes.

Heat the remaining olive oil in a pan, add the breadcrumbs and cook over low heat, stirring constantly, until the breadcrumbs are golden. (Add a little more oil if the breadcrumbs are too dry.)

Stir in the chopped parsley and remove the pan from the heat.

Beat the eggs with the cream, mustard and salt and pepper to taste. Pour the egg mixture over the vegetables and top with the golden breadcrumbs.

Bake for about 35 minutes, until the eggs are set.

Remove the dish from the oven and let stand until the gratin is warm rather than hot, then serve.

Courgette (Zucchini) & Tomato Gratin

{ Green Tarts }

Tarts

Our tarts are always the most popular items on our counter at lunchtime, and have been ever since we opened. They include eggs in the pastry dough and in the cream mixture that forms the basis of the fillings. We make a huge variety of fillings with different combinations of vegetables, herbs and meats – these recipes are just a small selection of what we do, so you must feel free to experiment with different fillings.

BASIC PASTRY DOUGH

Our vegetable tarts remain very popular and are relatively easy to make. This pastry dough is perfect for quiches and vegetable tarts. I included the recipe in my first book and am happy to repeat it here.

Makes 3 x 28 cm (11 inch) tarts or 12 x 8–10 cm (3¼–4 inch) individual tarts

500 g (4½ cups) **plain** (all-purpose) **flour**
1 teaspoon salt
250 g (generous 1 cup) **unsalted butter**
1 egg yolk
125–250 ml (½–1 cup) **water**

Sift the flour and salt into a bowl, add the butter and rub in with your fingertips until the mixture resembles fresh breadcrumbs.

Make a well in the middle and add the egg yolk and 125 ml (½ cup) water.

Mix vigorously with a fork until almost all the flour is incorporated, then add a little more water and bring the dough together with your fingers, using as little water as possible. The dough should just come together naturally without force, and be soft but firm and not sticky.

Shape into a ball, wrap in clingfilm (plastic wrap) and chill in the refrigerator for at least 30 minutes.

GREEN TARTS

This great restorative one-pot dish is good way to use up extra vegetables.

Makes 12 x 8–10 cm (3¼–4 inch) individual tarts

butter, for greasing
1 quantity Basic Pastry Dough (see page 65)
plain (all-purpose) **flour, for dusting**

For the filling

2 tablespoons Dijon mustard
1.5 litres (6¼ cups) **single** (light) **cream**
8 eggs
2 egg yolks
½ teaspoon salt
pinch of grated nutmeg
250 g (2¼ cups) **grated Cheddar cheese**
2 heads broccoli, blanched, drained and broken into small florets
2 handfuls shredded spinach
1 bunch fresh chives, chopped
ground black pepper

Grease 12 x 8–10 cm (3¼–4 inch) individual tart pans with butter.

Roll out the dough to about 5 mm (⅛ inch) thick on a lightly floured surface and cut 12 rounds to fit the prepared tart pans. Ease them into the tart pans and trim off any excess dough. Let rest in the refrigerator for 30 minutes.

Preheat the oven to 180°C/350°F/Gas Mark 4. Then line the pastry cases (shells) with foil or greaseproof (wax paper) and fill with dried beans, baking beans (pie weights) or rice.

Bake blind for 30–35 minutes, until the base is light, golden and dry. Remove from the oven, take out the weights and lining and let cool.

To make the filling, beat together the mustard, cream, eggs, egg yolks, salt, nutmeg and pepper to taste in a bowl.

Preheat the oven to 180°C/350°F/Gas Mark 4.

Divide the cheese among the pastry cases. Mix the broccoli florets and spinach together and divide the mixture among the pastry cases. Cover with the egg mixture and top each tart with a generous sprinkling of chives. (The green of the broccoli florets and spinach must stick out so the impression is of lots of greens.)

Bake for 25 minutes, until set and golden.

Remove from the oven and serve immediately or let cool.

LEEK & MUSTARD TARTS

Sometimes we cover these tarts with a sprinkling of crisply fried fresh breadcrumbs for extra crunch.

Makes 12 x 8–10 cm (3¼–4 inch) individual tarts

butter, for greasing
1 quantity Basic Pastry Dough (see page 65)
plain (all-purpose) **flour, for dusting**

For the filling

4 tablespoons virgin olive oil
6–8 leeks, thinly sliced
1 teaspoon sugar
½ teaspoon salt
2 tablespoons Dijon mustard
1.5 litres (6¼ cups) **single** (light) **cream**
8 eggs
2 egg yolks
pinch of grated nutmeg
250 g (2¼ cups) **grated Cheddar cheese**
3 tomatoes, sliced
ground black pepper

Grease 12 x 8–10 cm (3¼–4 inch) individual tart pans with butter.

Roll out the dough to about 5 mm (⅛ inch) thick on a lightly floured surface and cut 12 rounds to fit the prepared tart pans. Ease them into the tart pans and trim off any excess dough. Let rest in the refrigerator for 30 minutes.

Preheat the oven to 180°C/350°F/Gas Mark 4. Then line the pastry cases (shells) with foil or greaseproof (wax paper) and fill with dried beans, baking beans (pie weights) or rice.

Bake blind for 30–35 minutes, until the base is light, golden and dry. Remove from the oven, take out the weights and lining and let cool.

To make the filling, heat the oil in a pan, add the leeks, sprinkle with the sugar and ½ teaspoon salt, season with pepper and cook over low heat, stirring occasionally, for 15 minutes, until softened. Remove the pan from the heat.

Beat together the mustard, cream, eggs, egg yolks, nutmeg, ½ teaspoon salt and pepper to taste in a bowl.

Preheat the oven to 180°C/350°F/Gas Mark 4.

When the pastry cases are cold, divide the grated cheese among them, then add the leeks. Top with the tomato slices and cover with the egg mixture, filling them as high as you dare go without spilling.

Bake for about 25 minutes, until set and golden.

Remove from the oven and serve immediately or let cool.

CURRIED CAULIFLOWER TARTS

You can vary the vegetables used in the filling for these tarts and replace the potatoes with roast pumpkin or even cooked okra (ladies' fingers) or peas.

Makes 12 x 8–10 cm (3¼–4 inch) individual tarts

butter, for greasing
1 quantity Basic Pastry Dough (see page 65)
plain (all-purpose) **flour, for dusting**

For the filling

1 tablespoon curry powder
1.5 litres (6¼ cups) **single** (light) **cream**
2 tablespoons Dijon mustard
8 eggs
2 egg yolks
pinch of grated nutmeg
½ teaspoon salt
250 g (2¼ cups) **grated Cheddar cheese**
2–3 heads cauliflower, blanched, drained and broken into small florets
500 g (1 pound 2 ounces) **potatoes diced, boiled and drained**
1 bunch fresh coriander (cilantro)**, coarsely chopped**
ground black pepper

Grease 12 x 8–10 cm (3¼–4 inch) individual tart pans with butter.

Roll out the dough to about 5 mm (⅛ inch) thick on a lightly floured surface and cut 12 rounds to fit the prepared tart pans. Ease them into the tart pans and trim off any excess dough. Let rest in the refrigerator for 30 minutes.

Preheat the oven to 180°C/350°F/Gas Mark 4. Then line the pastry cases (shells) with foil or greaseproof (wax paper) and fill with dried beans, baking beans (pie weights) or rice.

Bake blind for 30–35 minutes, until the base is light, golden and dry. Remove from the oven, take out the weights and lining and let cool.

Meanwhile, stir the curry powder into the cream, then beat in the mustard, eggs, egg yolks, nutmeg, ½ teaspoon salt and pepper to taste in a bowl.

Preheat the oven to 180°C/350°F/Gas Mark 4.

Divide the cheese among the pastry cases (shells), then add the cauliflower florets, diced potatoes and most of the coriander. Cover with the egg mixture and top with the remaining coriander.

Bake for about 25 minutes, until firm and golden.

Remove from the oven and serve immediately or let cool.

{ Tarragon Chicken }

Main Courses

We always have one or two main courses on our lunch menu at Rose Bakery. As we have so many eggs on our breakfast menu, they are not always central to our our lunch dishes, but many of them use eggs either as a binder for the sauce, or as a garnish.

TARRAGON CHICKEN

This is a wonderful dish for a hot summer's day, as you prepare it the day before and eat it cold. It was inspired by cookery writer Elizabeth David's *Poulet à la Crème et à l'Estragon*, but I have adapted it to make it easier, with only chicken breasts rather than a whole chicken.

Serves 4

4 chicken breasts, skinned
olive oil, for drizzling
500 ml (2¼ cups) **good-quality home-made**
  chicken stock
100 ml (scant ½ cup) **whipping cream**
8 egg yolks, beaten
1 bunch fresh tarragon, chopped
1–2 teaspoons lemon juice
salt and ground black pepper
green salad, potato salad or sliced tomatoes,
  to serve

Preheat the oven to 180°C/350°F/Gas mark 4.

Put the chicken breasts in an ovenproof dish, drizzle with olive oil and season with salt and pepper.

Roast for 12–15 minutes, until the flesh is firm to the touch. Remove from the oven and let cool.

Meanwhile, pour the stock into a pan and bring to a boil. Reduce the heat to low, stir in the cream, egg yolks and half the tarragon and cook, stirring constantly with a wooden spoon, until the sauce coats the spoon. Do not let the mixture boil, as this will make the eggs curdle.

Remove the pan from the heat and strain into a bowl, then season to taste with salt and pepper and stir in lemon juice to taste.

Pour the sauce over the chicken and sprinkle with the remaining tarragon.

Cover with clingfilm (plastic wrap) and chill in the refrigerator overnight.

The sauce will thicken and set to a soft mayonnaise.

Serve chilled with a green salad, potato salad or some sliced tomatoes.

MEATBALLS

Serves 6

6 tablespoons olive oil
3 onions, finely diced
2 slices bread, crusts removed
3 tablespoons milk
800 g (1¾ pounds) **minced** (ground) **beef**
2–3 garlic cloves, mashed
3–4 tablespoons chopped fresh flat-leaf parsley,
   plus extra to garnish (optional)
2 tablespoons grated Parmesan cheese,
   plus extra to garnish (optional)
2 eggs
salt and ground black pepper
spaghetti or rice, to serve

For the tomato sauce

2 tablespoons olive oil
1 onion, diced
pinch of sugar
pinch of chilli flakes (optional)
2 garlic cloves, mashed
5 tomatoes, peeled, seeded and diced,
   or 400 g (14 ounces) **canned tomatoes**
1 tablespoon tomato purée (paste)
handful of fresh basil leaves
salt and ground black pepper

First make the tomato sauce. Heat the oil in a pan, add the onion and cook over low heat, stirring occasionally, for 5–8 minutes, until softened but not brown. Stir in the sugar and chilli, if using, season with salt and pepper and add the garlic, tomatoes, tomato purée, basil and 120 ml (½ cup) water.

Simmer, stirring occasionally, for about 20 minutes, until thickened and glossy. Remove the pan from the heat and set aside.

To make the meatballs, heat 2 tablespoons of the oil in a small pan, add the onions and cook over low heat, stirring occasionally, for 5–8 minutes, until softened but not brown.

Meanwhile, tear the bread into pieces, put it into a bowl, add the milk and let soak.

When the onions are soft, remove from the heat and let cool slightly. Put the onions, minced beef, garlic, parsley, Parmesan and eggs in a bowl.

Squeeze out the bread, add it to the bowl, season with salt and pepper and mix well using your hands.

It is always best to fry a small amount to taste the seasoning – we find it always needs more salt and pepper. When you are satisfied with the seasoning, shape the mixture into balls about the size of golf balls.

Heat the remaining oil in a pan, add the meatballs and cook, turning occasionally, until browned all over. Add the tomato sauce and simmer for at least 45 minutes so that all the flavours meld.

Serve hot with spaghetti or rice and top with extra chopped parsley or Parmesan cheese.

TOFU BALLS

There are probably as many meatball recipes in the world as there are cooks. Some of them contain eggs, others not. It's all down to traditions and personal preferences. I thought I would include a recipe for tofu balls as this is a little more unusual.

Serves 4

6 tablespoons olive oil
1 onion, finely diced and softened in olive oil
400 g (14 ounces) **firm tofu, mashed**
50 g (½ cup) **coarsely ground walnuts**
25 g (½ cup) **fine fresh breadcrumbs**
2 eggs
3–4 tablespoons chopped fresh flat-leaf parsley
pinch of chilli flakes
salt and ground black pepper
1 quantity Tomato Sauce (see Meatballs), made
   with fresh oregano instead of basil, to serve

Heat 2 tablespoons of the oil in a pan, add the onion and cook over low heat, stirring occasionally, for 5–8 minutes, until softened but not brown.

Remove from the heat and let cool slightly.

Mix together the onion, tofu, walnuts, breadcrumbs, eggs, parsley, chilli and salt and pepper to taste in a bowl until thoroughly combined. Add more breadcrumbs if the mixture is too wet.

Form into 3 cm (1¼ inch) balls with your hands.

Heat the remaining olive oil in a frying pan or skillet, add the tofu balls and cook, turning frequently, until golden brown and cooked through.

Remove with a slotted spoon and serve with tomato and oregano sauce.

LENTIL & WHOLE GRAIN FRITTERS

Here I am using a combination of lentils, barley and brown rice, but you could use a combination of any other grains if you wish, such as spelt, wheatberries or millet, and substitute brown lentils for the green. I just love barley, so anything with that is fine by me. I like to serve these fritters with tomato salad and topped with extra herbs.

Serves 4

60 g (¼ cup) **pot** (whole grain) **barley,
  soaked overnight in cold water and drained**
50 g (¼ cup) **brown rice**
60 g (¼ cup) **green lentils**
1 tablespoon olive oil, plus extra for pan-frying
2 onions, diced
1 teaspoon sugar
2 garlic cloves, mashed
2 eggs
50 ml (¼ cup) **milk**
25 g (¼ cup) **wholemeal** (whole wheat) **flour mixed
  with ½ teaspoon baking powder**
40 g (½ cup) **grated Parmesan cheese**
3–4 tablespoons chopped fresh flat-leaf parsley
salt and ground black pepper

Put the barley into a pan, pour in 250 ml (1 cup) water and simmer for 30–45 minutes, until tender.

Meanwhile, put the rice into another pan, pour in 250 ml (1 cup) water and simmer for 35–45 minutes, until tender.

Put the lentils into a third pan, pour in 250 ml (1 cup) water and simmer for about 30 minutes, until just tender.

As the grains and lentils are ready, season and drain. Heat the oil in a frying pan or skillet, add the onions and cook over medium-low heat for 10–12 minutes, until softened and just beginning to turn golden.

Remove from the heat, season with the sugar, a pinch of salt and pepper, add the garlic and let cool.

Put the barley, rice, lentils, onion mixture, eggs, milk, flour and Parmesan into a bowl and mix together, then fold in the parsley. (Do not mix too much – the mixture should be similar to a pancake batter. Add more milk if it is too stiff or more flour if it is too wet.)

Heat a little olive oil in a frying pan or skillet over medium heat. When hot, drop tablespoons of the mixture into the pan making sure they are well spaced out.

Cook until bubbles start to appear on the surface, then turn over carefully, checking the heat to make sure it is not cooking too slowly or too fast. Cook for a few minutes more until cooked through. Remove the fritters with a spatula and keep warm while you cook the remaining mixture in the same way.

BUCKWHEAT CRÊPES

These can be served with many savoury options such as smoked fish, crab meat, or grilled with cheese, ham, and any vegetable of your choice.

Makes about 15

3 eggs
250 ml (1 cup) **buttermilk or thin plain yogurt**
250 ml (1 cup) **beer**
60 g (4½ tablespoons) **butter, melted**
40–80 g (⅓–¾ cup) **buckwheat flour**
40 g (⅓ cup) **plain** (all-purpose) **flour**
1 teaspoon baking powder
¼ teaspoon bicarbonate of soda (baking soda)
2 teaspoons sugar
¼ teaspoon salt
vegetable oil, for brushing

Beat the eggs in a bowl, then add the buttermilk, beer and melted butter.

Mix together the dry ingredients in another bowl, then pour the egg mixture into the dry ingredients and mix well.

Cover and chill in the refrigerator for at least 1 hour.

Brush a frying pan or skillet or griddle (grill) pan with a little oil and heat. When the pan is hot, pour in just enough batter to cover the bottom thinly and cook until the edge starts to turn golden and dry.

Turn the crêpe with a spatula, cook for another few minutes, then slide it out of the pan onto a plate.

Keep warm while you cook more crêpes in same way, brushing the pan with more oil as necessary, until all the batter has been used.

THREE-COLOURED FRITTATA

This recipe slightly contradicts everything I've said about using eggs simply, but I feel it will appeal to anyone wanting something pretty or different. A frittata or tortilla is basically a flat omelette with vegetables scattered on top or within the egg mixture to form a savoury cake. It is delicious, whether served hot or cold.

Serves 1–2

4 eggs
4 tablespoons roasted red bell pepper purée
4 tablespoons spinach purée
2 tablespoons olive oil
salt and ground black pepper
green salad, to serve

Preheat the oven to 180°C/350°F/Gas Mark 4.

Lightly beat the eggs in a bowl and season with salt and pepper.

Divide into 3 equal parts in 3 separate bowls.

Stir the red bell pepper purée into one bowl and the spinach purée into another, leaving the third plain.

From here on be as creative as you like.

Heat the olive oil in a frying pan or skillet with an ovenproof handle over high heat. When it's hot, reduce the heat to medium and pour the plain eggs, then the red mixture and, finally, the green one over the base of the pan, creating a crazy or simple design.

If the pan is too hot, take it off the heat while you do this.

Transfer the pan to the oven for a few minutes until the egg has set, as a frittata must cook slowly. This will also make sure that the underside doesn't burn.

Serve immediately with a light green salad.

{ Three-Coloured Frittata }

LACY EGGS OVER VEGETABLES

You will need a great vegetable stew for this dish. I have suggested a basic slightly curried version, but you can add courgettes (zucchini), celery, parsnips and anything you like. A delicious ratatouille is just as good or you can simply combine your favourite vegetables.

Serves 4

1–2 tablespoons olive oil
1 onion, diced
1 leek, thinly sliced
1–2 dried chillies, crushed
2 garlic cloves, mashed
1 heaped teaspoon curry powder
pinch of sugar (optional)
2 tomatoes, peeled, seeded and diced
1 small head of cauliflower, cut into
small florets
300 ml (1¼ cups) **vegetable stock**
3–4 tablespoons chopped fresh coriander
(cilantro)
2 eggs
salt and ground black pepper

Heat 1½ tablespoons of the oil in a pan, add the onion and cook over low heat, stirring occasionally, for 5–8 minutes, until softened.

Add the leek and chillies, season with salt and pepper and continue cooking gently, stirring occasionally, until soft.

Add the garlic, stir in the curry powder and add the sugar, if you want to take away the bitterness of the curry.

Add the tomatoes and cook until most of the liquid has evaporated, then add the cauliflower florets and vegetable stock. Continue to cook gently until most of the stock has cooked off and the cauliflower is tender.

Taste and adjust the seasoning, if necessary, and add the chopped coriander. Keep warm while you prepare the eggs.

Lightly beat the eggs in a jug (pitcher) without making them frothy.

Heat the remaining olive oil in a frying pan or skillet over medium heat. When the pan is hot, reduce the heat and wipe off excess oil with paper towels.

Drizzle in some of the beaten egg to create a lace pattern – it will cook very quickly.

Lift out carefully with a spatula and keep warm while you cook the remaining egg in the same way.

Divide the vegetable stew among 4 plates or bowls, top with the egg lace and serve.

ROSE BAKERY RATATOUILLE

I've had many requests to add this simple summer stew to our list of recipes. It is truly a wonderful accompaniment to poached or fried eggs and is also great with Lacy Eggs.

3 courgettes (zucchini)**, cut into chunks**
2 aubergines (eggplants)**, cut into chunks**
120 ml (½ cup) **olive oil**
3 onions, chopped
pinch of chilli flakes
1 red bell pepper, half peeled, seeded and diced
5 very ripe tomatoes, peeled, seeded and
coarsely chopped, or 800 g (1¾ pounds) **canned**
tomatoes, coarsely chopped, or a combination
of both, coarsely chopped
3 garlic cloves, mashed
1 teaspoon sugar
handful of fresh basil leaves, torn (optional)
salt and ground black pepper

Preheat the oven to 180°C/350°F/Gas Mark 4.

Put the courgettes and aubergines into separate ovenproof dishes, drizzle with olive oil, season with salt and pepper and roast for 25–30 minutes, until tender and golden.

Meanwhile, heat the remaining olive oil in a large pan, add the onions and cook over low heat, stirring occasionally, for 5–8 minutes, until softened.

Sprinkle with the chilli, season with salt, add the bell pepper and continue cooking for an additional 5–8 minutes, until softened.

Stir in the tomatoes, garlic, sugar and 120 ml (½ cup) water and simmer for about 35 minutes, until the sauce is reduced, rich and shiny.

Taste and adjust the seasoning, if necessary.

Remove the courgettes and aubergines from the oven, tip them into the pan and mix well. If you like, you can transfer the mixture to an ovenproof dish and roast for about 15 minutes more.

Let the ratatouille stand until it is warm, rather than hot, fold in the basil leaves and serve.

Ratatouille improves with keeping – it tastes even better the next day, but never serve it straight from the refrigerator.

MASHED POTATOES, EGGS & PARMESAN

This is comfort food at its best. For it to be perfect you must have the best mashed potatoes, so you will need suitable varieties: in Ireland you will have Golden Wonders, in France Bintje, in the UK Desiree, in the US Yukon Gold, and so on. As long as the potatoes are not waxy they will be fine.

I cook them whole without peeling them, to keep as much water out as possible, simmering them gently until they are soft.

Drain them and, as soon as possible, peel them. Start mashing, adding butter or olive oil or full-fat (whole) milk and season with salt and ground black pepper. This must be done while the potatoes are still warm. I like them fluffy and light with olive oil, but you may prefer them creamy and full of butter.

As soon as they are to your taste, serve.

For this dish I put a mound of mashed potatoes on the plate, top with poached or fried (see page 19) eggs and finished with a generous grating of Parmesan cheese. Total bliss.

Variations

You can add lots of different ingredients to the mashed potatoes. These are some of my favourites:

– Saffron soaked in a little hot water
– Lots of chopped fresh herbs, such as chives
– Garlic mashed into a little warm cream
– Cooked and puréed artichoke hearts

SPINACH & RICOTTA GNOCCHI

A light tomato sauce, preferably made with fresh tomatoes, is the perfect partner for these gnocchi. However, if you do not have a tomato sauce to hand, they are also great with melted butter and extra spinach.

Serves 4

500 g (2½ cups) **ricotta cheese**
40 g (1½ ounces) **Parmesan cheese, plus extra to serve**
2 eggs
3–4 tablespoons plain (all-purpose) **flour**
large pinch of grated nutmeg
200 g (2⅓ cups) **chopped cooked spinach, squeezed dry**
salt and ground black pepper
1 quantity Tomato Sauce (see page 70), to serve

Mix together all the ingredients, except the tomato sauce, to form a soft dough. If it is too soft to roll out, add a little more flour.

Cover and chill in the refrigerator for 1 hour.

Divide the dough into 3 equal pieces. Roll each piece into a sausage-shape about 3 cm (1¼ inches) in diameter. Cut into 3 cm (1½ inch) slices.

Using a fork, press lightly on each gnocchi to make a slight groove, if you like. (The gnocchi can be kept for a few hours in the refrigerator if you don't want to cook them immediately.)

Bring a large pan of salted water to a boil, then reduce the heat to a simmer.

Drop the gnocchi into the simmering water, in batches, and cook for a few minutes until they rise to the surface.

Remove with a slotted spoon and keep warm while you cook the remaining batches.

Serve immediately topped with tomato sauce and extra Parmesan cheese.

{ Traditional Chawanmushi }

Savoury Custards

I love the savoury custards that are served in Japanese restaurants. They are called chawanmushi (literally 'steamed in a tea bowl') and are made in little bowls with lids. I'm sure we have another name for them in our Western cooking repertoire, but whatever they are called, they are so delicious and can be altered to suit your tastes and diet.

TRADITIONAL CHAWANMUSHI

Chawanmushi is often served as an appetizer instead of soup, but I could easily eat it on its own. You will need 4 pretty cups or heatproof bowls and a steamer or a large casserole (dutch oven) or pan with a lid.

Serves 4

4 eggs
600 ml (2½ cups) **dashi (see page 12) or other stock**
1 teaspoon shoyu (see page 13)
1 teaspoon sugar
dash of sake (optional)
4 fresh shitake mushrooms, trimmed and thinly sliced
about 150 g (5 ounces) **skinless, boneless chicken breast, cut into bite-size pieces**
8 cooked prawns (shrimp)**, shelled**
8 mangetouts (snow peas) **or pieces of spinach**
salt
chopped fresh chives or spring onions (scallions)**, to garnish (optional)**

Lightly mix the eggs with a fork in a bowl, taking care not to make them frothy.

Add the stock, shoyu, sugar and sake, if using. Taste and season with salt if necessary.

Strain the mixture into a jug (pitcher). Divide the mushrooms, chicken, prawns and mangetouts among 4 heatproof bowls or cups.

Pour water into the base of a steamer or large casserole to a depth of about 4 cm (1½ inches) and heat. Put the cups into the steamer and fill with the egg mixture. Cover the steamer with a dish towel and lid. If using a casserole, cover each cup with clingfilm (plastic wrap) and put the lid on.

Steam over high heat for about 2 minutes, then reduce the heat to low and continue steaming for an additional 20 minutes, until a cocktail stick or toothpick inserted into the custard comes out clean. If there are still traces of the mixture, steam the custards for a little longer and test again.

Serve immediately, garnished with chives or spring onions if you like.

MY CHAWANMUSHI WITH
SPRING VEGETABLES

You will need 4 pretty cups or heatproof bowls and a steamer or a large casserole (dutch oven) or pan with a lid.

Serves 4

4 eggs
600 ml (2½ cups) **vegetable stock**
1 teaspoon shoyu (see page 13)
1 teaspoon sugar
pinch of cayenne pepper
½ head broccoli, cut into florets, blanched
  and drained
80 g (¾ cup) **cooked peas**
4 spring onions (scallions)**, very thinly sliced**
4 shiitake or other mushroom, thinly sliced
handful of spinach or other tender greens
1 carrot, sliced into rounds, blanched
  and drained
salt
chopped fresh herbs, to garnish

Lightly mix the eggs with a fork in a bowl, taking care not to make them frothy.

Add the stock, shoyu, sugar and cayenne pepper. Taste and season with salt if necessary.

Strain the mixture into a jug (pitcher). Divide the vegetables among 4 heatproof bowls or cups.

Pour water into the base of a steamer or large casserole to a depth of about 4 cm (1½ inches) and heat. Put the cups into the steamer and fill with the egg mixture. Cover the steamer with a dish towel and lid. If using a casserole, cover each cup with clingfilm (plastic wrap) and put the lid on.

Steam over high heat for about 2 minutes, then reduce the heat to low and continue steaming for an additional 20 minutes, until a cocktail stick or toothpick inserted into the custard comes out clean. If there are still traces of the mixture, steam the custards for a little longer and test again.

Garnish with chopped herbs of your choice and serve immediately.

MY CHAWANMUSHI WITH SEAFOOD

You will need 4 pretty cups or heatproof bowls and a steamer or a large casserole (dutch oven) or pan with a lid. You can add some of the liquid from cooking the mussels to the stock if it's not too salty.

Serves 4

5 eggs
600 ml (2½ cups) **dashi (see page 12)**
  or vegetable stock
1 teaspoon shoyu (see page 13)
1 teaspoon sugar
1 teaspoon grated lemon zest
3–4 tablespoons chopped fresh chives
12 cooked mussels, shelled
200 g (7 ounces) **salmon or white fish fillet,**
  cut into bite-size pieces
4 cooked prawns (shrimp)**, shelled**
2 tomatoes, peeled, seeded and finely diced
1 courgette (zucchini)**, thinly sliced**
salt

Lightly mix the eggs with a fork in a bowl, taking care not to make them frothy.

Add the stock, shoyu, sugar and lemon zest. Taste and season with salt if necessary.

Strain the mixture into a jug (pitcher). Reserve some of the chives for the garnish and divide the remainder, together with the seafood and vegetables, between 2 heatproof bowls.

Pour water into the base of a steamer or large casserole to a depth of about 4 cm (1½ inches) and heat. Put the bowls into the steamer and fill with the egg mixture. Cover the steamer with a dish towel and lid. If using a casserole, cover each bowl with clingfilm (plastic wrap) and put the lid on.

Steam over high heat for about 2 minutes, then reduce the heat to low and continue steaming for an additional 20–30 minutes, until a cocktail stick or toothpick inserted into the custard comes out clean. If there are still traces of the mixture, steam the custards for a little longer and test again.

Serve garnished with the reserved chives.

{ My Chawanmushi
with Spring Vegetables }

{ Our Salad Niçoise }

Salads

Eggs are used in many classic salads such as Niçoise, Caesar, potato, and the wonderful leeks mimosa. There is much debate about what goes into a Niçoise or Caesar salad, but, once again, it's all down to personal tastes and preferences, unless you are a stickler for authenticity. The following recipes are my favourites.

OUR SALAD NIÇOISE

The term *niçoise* is used rather vaguely to describe a salad made from ingredients commonly found in the region around Nice in southern France. We just use it to describe our vegetable salad that includes olives and eggs. There are not really any hard-and-fast rules and you can use almost any vegetable you like. A combination of raw and cooked vegetables is especially nice.

Serves 4

200 g (7 ounces) **fine green beans**
3 tablespoons lemon juice
4 small globe artichokes
3 tablespoons olive oil
100 g (3½ ounces) **mixed salad leaves** (greens)
4 tomatoes, sliced, halved, or cut into wedges
2 small red onions, very thinly sliced
4–5 red radishes, very thinly sliced
120 g (4 ounces) **white tuna canned in oil, drained and flaked**
50 g (½ cup) **black olives**
2 hard-boiled eggs (see page 19), shelled and quartered
about 200 ml (scant 1 cup) **Vinaigrette (see page 82)**

Cook the green beans in boiling water for 4–5 minutes, until tender but still crisp, then drain and set aside.

Half-fill a bowl with water and stir in the lemon juice.

Remove the tough outer leaves from the artichokes by snapping them off at the base to reveal the paler inner part. Slice off the top third of the artichokes, cut the stems to about 2 cm (¾ inch) and peel with a paring knife. Cut the artichokes in half lengthways and remove the hairy chokes. As each artichoke is prepared put it into the bowl of acidulated water to stop it from going brown.

Heat the olive oil in a frying pan or skillet.

Drain the artichokes, pat dry and slice quite thinly, then add to the pan and cook until golden. Remove from the pan, drain on paper towels and set aside.

Put the salad leaves into a large wide bowl and arrange all the vegetables as you wish, ending with the flaked tuna, olives and eggs.

Serve with the vinaigrette on the side.

EGG & CRESS SALAD

This has to be a marriage made in heaven. The combination of hard-boiled eggs and watercress in sandwiches has always been my favourite. It must be something to do with the peppery hotness of watercress and the soft chalkiness of the eggs. This salad version does not include mayonnaise, as the eggs mixed with the vinaigrette are perfect without it.

If watercress is unavailable, you could substitute another peppery salad green, such as rocket (arugula).

Serves 4

4 hard-boiled eggs (see page 19)
4 large handfuls watercress
3 spring onions (scallions)**, thinly sliced**
1 carton of mustard and cress
handful of croûtons, preferably roasted in
 olive oil

For the vinaigrette

3 tablespoons red wine vinegar
120 ml (1 cup) **olive oil**
1 tablespoon Dijon mustard
½ teaspoon salt
1 teaspoon clear honey
ground black pepper

Mix together all the ingredients for the vinaigrette and set aside.

Shell and coarsely chop the eggs and put them into a large salad bowl with the watercress, spring onions, mustard and cress and croûtons.

Pour the dressing over the salad, toss lightly and serve immediately.

Do not leave the salad standing around once the dressing has been added.

{ Egg & Cress Salad }

EGG SALAD WITH ARAME & RICE

Arame, a slightly sweet Japanese seaweed, is available in dried form from Japanese supermarkets and wholefood stores. It looks like a nest of fine, dark strips.

Serves 4

handful of dried arame (see page 12), soaked in 500 ml (2¼ cups) **warm water for 10 minutes**
1 tablespoon sesame oil, plus extra for drizzling
2 tablespoons soy sauce
2 heaped tablespoons sugar
4 hard-boiled eggs (see page 19)
500 g (3 cups) **cooked brown rice**
2–3 tablespoons toasted sesame seeds
2 spring onions (scallions)**, thinly sliced**
dash of rice wine vinegar

Wash the arame, then soak them in about 500 ml (2¼ cups) warm water for around 10 minutes until they have swollen to at least double their size. Drain and reserve the soaking liquid.

Heat the sesame oil in a pan, add the arame and cook for a few minutes.

Add the soy sauce and enough of the reserved soaking liquid just to cover the arame. Add the sugar, bring to a boil, reduce the heat and simmer until nearly all the liquid has evaporated.

Remove the pan from the heat and set aside.

Shell the eggs and cut them into wedges or slices, then mix with the arame, brown rice, sesame seeds and spring onions in a salad bowl.

Drizzle with sesame oil, add a splash of rice wine vinegar and serve.

Even though this salad keeps well for a few hours in the refrigerator, it is best served as soon after making as possible.

CAULIFLOWER & EGG CURRY SALAD

I love this salad with boiled eggs, but you also use fine omelettes rolled and cut into 'noodles' (see page 56) or even poached eggs (see page 19).

While I'm on the subject, there is nothing more wonderful than warm potatoes and a great vinaigrette, topped with poached eggs and sprinkled with chives. Poached or soft-boiled eggs marry well with any leaf salad too, as long as they are eaten immediately and combined with a good dressing. There is something about eggs and vinegar... and this takes me back to the Scrambled Eggs & Vinegar recipe (see page 29). Makes sense.

Serves 4

2 tablespoons olive oil
50 g (1 cup) **fine fresh breadcrumbs**
1 large cauliflower, broken into small florets, blanched for a few minutes and drained
4 hard-boiled eggs (see page 19), shelled and chopped
chopped fresh coriander (cilantro)**, to garnish**

For the vinaigrette

1 shallot, finely diced
½ teaspoon salt
1 teaspoon curry powder
3 tablespoons white wine vinegar
5 tablespoons light olive oil or rapeseed (canola) **oil**
pinch of sugar (optional)
ground black pepper

First make the vinaigrette. Mix together the shallot, salt, curry powder, vinegar and oil and season with pepper. Taste, and if is too bitter, add the sugar. Set aside.

Heat the olive oil in a pan, add the breadcrumbs and cook over low heat, stirring constantly, until they are golden. (Add a little more oil if the breadcrumbs are too dry.)

Remove from the heat.

Put the cauliflower, egg and crispy breadcrumbs into a bowl, pour the vinaigrette over and lightly mix together. A handful of chopped coriander is a nice garnish.

LEEK VINAIGRETTE WITH EGGS & HERBS

This has to be one of my favourite ways to eat leeks. When we are in deep winter and the asparagus season seems so far away, this dish just cheers me up. Be very careful to choose thin leeks, no more than 2 cm (¾ inch) thick.

Serves 4

12 leeks trimmed, leaving about 3 cm (1¼ inches) **of green on each**
400 ml (1¾ cups) **olive oil, plus extra for drizzling**
2 tablespoons Dijon mustard
3 tablespoons white or red wine vinegar
2 hard-boiled eggs (see page 19), shelled and coarsely chopped
handful mixed chopped fresh flat-leaf parsley and chives
salt and ground black pepper

Preheat the oven to 180°C/350°F/Gas Mark 4.

Put the leeks in an ovenproof dish with about 1 cm (½ inch) water, drizzle with olive oil and season with salt and pepper.

Cover with foil and bake for about 20 minutes, until a knife goes in easily. The leeks should be just cooked through, but not soft.

Remove from the oven, drain off the water and let cool.

Meanwhile, make the vinaigrette. Whisk together the mustard, vinegar and a pinch of salt and pepper in a bowl. Add the olive oil and whisk a little more. Taste and adjust the seasoning, if necessary, and add more oil if the vinegar is too sharp or more vinegar if the oil is overwhelming.

Transfer the leeks to 4 individual plates and sprinkle with the chopped eggs and herbs.

Put the vinaigrette in a sauceboat or drizzle it over the leeks, then serve immediately.

{ Egg Sandwich }

Light Lunches

Whenever we make sandwiches, which is not as often as we would like, they disappear much faster than anything else, and the same applies to our scotch eggs. I love sandwiches for lunch and any egg sandwich has to be the best. They are so versatile that there are an infinite number of variations, but these are a few that I particularly like.

EGG SANDWICH

I have a wonderful memory of walking round Berkeley, California with our young children and friends and suddenly realizing how hungry we all were, but not knowing where to go to eat. Fortunately we came across the newly opened Fanny's Café. I can't remember what the kids had but we adults were completely satisfied with the most memorable open sandwich ever and it was simplicity itself.

The bread for sandwiches should always be very special. Sourdough is an excellent choice. Mix chopped hard-boiled eggs (see page 19) with just a touch of mayonnaise (see page 21) and season with salt and pepper to taste. Divide among the slices of bread and top with watercress or sprouting cress. You can also add very fine slivers of canned anchovy if you like. I can't think of a more satisfying light lunch.

CLUB SANDWICH

You will need thinly sliced bread for this sandwich, otherwise the layers might get too high. Steamed eggs are cooked using the steamer tube on our coffee machines, but if you don't have this option, soft scrambled eggs are just as good.

Serves 1

3 thin slices freshly toasted bread, preferably sourdough
steamed or scrambled eggs (see page 19)
1–2 slices prosciutto
rocket (arugula) **leaves, to taste**
olive oil, for drizzling
salt and ground black pepper

Spoon the eggs over one slice of toast and top with the second slice.

Put the prosciutto and rocket on top, season with salt and pepper and drizzle with olive oil.

Cover with the third slice of toast and cut the sandwich in half. It is really important to serve this sandwich while the toast is still warm.

OMELETTE SANDWICH

Again the bread is so important and my preference is always wholemeal (whole wheat).

Serves 1

butter or olive oil
2 slices wholemeal (whole wheat) **bread**
thin omelette (see page 19), seasoned with a pinch of cumin, smoked paprika or your favourite spice, folded in half
thinly sliced red onion, to taste
thinly sliced tomato, to taste
fresh coriander (cilantro) **or salad leaves, to taste**
salt and ground black pepper

Butter the bread or drizzle with olive oil.

Put the omelette on 1 slice, top with the onion, tomato and coriander or salad leaves, season well with salt and pepper and drizzle with olive oil.

Top with the other slice of bread.

CURRIED EGG SANDWICH

Curry spice and eggs is one of those marriages made in heaven. This recipe is inspired by the classic 'coronation' chicken sauce but without mayonnaise. The chopped hard-boiled eggs are rich enough to take on the curry!

Makes 2 sandwiches

4 tablespoons olive or rapeseed oil
1 medium onion, finely diced
1 teaspoon ground cumin
1 teaspoon ground coriander
½ teaspoon turmeric
pinch of cayenne pepper
1 tablespoon salt
1 large teaspoon apricot jam
4 hard-boiled eggs (see page 19), peeled
4 slices wholemeal (whole wheat) **or sourdough bread**
butter for spreading
2–3 spring onions (scallions)**, thinly sliced**
fresh coriander (cilantro) **leaves, to taste**

Heat the oil in a small frying pan and add the onion. Fry gently for about 5 minutes until the onion is very soft and just about to colour. Add the spices and salt and cook for another 2 minutes. Stir in the jam and about 75 ml (⅓ cup) water. Simmer on low heat for 4–5 minutes until thickened into a sort of syrup. Take off the heat and cool.

Chop the eggs roughly and pour over the sauce. Mix well and taste for seasoning.

Grill the bread on one side only, if possible. Butter the ungrilled sides and spread the egg mixture over two of the slices. Top with the chopped spring onion and the coriander and place the remaining slices of bread over the top, with the grilled sides up.

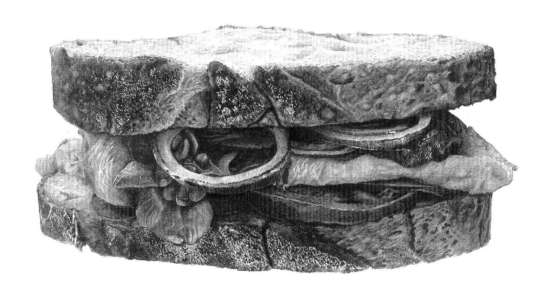

{ Omelette Sandwich }

{ Scotch Eggs }

SCOTCH EGGS

This traditional dish can be made more delicious if you prepare your own meat mix. However, if you know of an excellent home-made sausage from a good butcher, that will be fine too. We use panko breadcrumbs to coat our scotch eggs because they have a crisp, airy texture. They are available from Asian and Japanese food stores and increasingly from large supermarkets.

Makes 6

8 eggs
50 g (½ cup) **plain** (all-purpose) **flour**
65 g (1 cup) **panko breadcrumbs**
sunflower oil, frying
mustard, mayonnaise (see page 21) or salad,
  to serve

For the meat mixture

500 g (1 pound 2 ounces) **minced** (ground) **shoulder**
  (blade shoulder) **of pork including 100 g**
  (3½ ounces) **pork fat**
150 g (5 ounces) **bacon, finely diced**
1 egg
1 bunch fresh sage, chopped
1 bunch fresh flat-leaf parsley, chopped
1 teaspoon salt
¾ teaspoon ground black pepper
2 shallots, finely diced
1 teaspoon honey
25 g (½ cup) **fine fresh breadcrumbs**

First make the meat mixture by mixing all the ingredients together until thoroughly blended. Wrap in clingfilm (plastic wrap) and chill in the refrigerator for 1 hour.

Meanwhile, hard-boil 6 of the eggs (see page 19) and let cool, then shell them.

Divide the meat mixture into 6 portions and flatten out each portion into a round with your hands.

Roll a hard-boiled egg in the flour, place it on the meat patty and, with your fingers, bring up the meat to cover the egg completely, leaving no gaps. Repeat with the remaining eggs and meat.

Lightly beat the remaining eggs in a shallow dish and spread out the breadcrumbs in another shallow dish. Roll each meat-wrapped egg first in flour, then in beaten egg and, finally, in breadcrumbs to coat.

Pour sunflower oil into a pan to a depth of about 3 cm (1¼ inches). (It should not come more than halfway up the side of the pan.) Set over high heat and check the temperature by dipping some breadcrumbs in the oil, which will bubble if it is hot enough.

Reduce the heat to medium, add the eggs and cook, turning occasionally, for 10 minutes, until evenly golden. Remove and drain on paper towels.

Eat while still warm with mustard, mayonnaise or salad.

EGGS

FOR

TEA

CAKES

Pumpkin Cake
Purple Corn & Blueberry Cake
Wholemeal (Whole Wheat) & Walnut Cake
Classic Genoise Sponge
Sponge Fingers
Chocolate & Orange Polenta Cake
Green Tea Genoise
Welsh Tea Cakes

PUDDINGS

Semolina Pudding
Bread & Butter Pudding
Deep Custard Tarts
Soy Crème Caramel
Orange Crème Caramel
A Simple Apple Flan
Rose Bakery Chocolate Mousse
Pavlova
Eton Mess
Îles Flottantes

Afternoon tea has enjoyed a huge revival in popularity, and it is certainly Rose Bakery's busiest time of day. It is also when eggs really come into their own. We can prepare many meals without eggs, but cakes and puddings are much more difficult to make without them. They are used to give our cakes texture and form and sometimes to help them rise. They are also used to set our puddings and create meringues. Whether we use the yolks and whites together or separately, they both have very important functions and produce very different results, as well as being the key to many of our favourite desserts – from Bread & Butter Pudding *(see page 110)* to Rose Bakery Chocolate Mousse *(see page 114)*.

We aim to serve healthier desserts and cakes by reducing the sugar content as much as we dare and by adding nutritious ingredients that are experimental and beneficial to health, such as purple corn powder, lucuma, yacón syrup, coconut butter and green tea, as well as nuts and fruit. In addition to being 'good' for you, these make interesting cakes, such as Purple Corn & Blueberry Cake *(see page 98)* and Green Tea Genoise *(see page 103)*. They are available in specialist whole food stores and on the internet.

Cakes

Our cakes are the stars of our counters and always attract the attention of passers-by. We make between five and eight cakes each day and eggs are vital for all but the vegan ones. They add flavour, texture and richness to the batter, as well as helping to bind all the other ingredients together. We bake most of our cakes in long rectangular pans, which makes them easier to sell in slices. They also look lovely lined up on the counter but you can make them in whatever shape of pan you prefer.

PUMPKIN CAKE

Makes 1 x 27 cm (10¾ inch) round or 1 x 27 x 10 cm (10¾ x 4 inch) rectangular cake

butter, for greasing
275 g (2½ cups) **plain** (all-purpose) **flour**
1 teaspoon salt
2 teaspoons bicarbonate of soda (baking soda)
1 teaspoon mixed (apple pie) **spice**
1 teaspoon ground cinnamon
250 ml (1 cup) **olive oil**
350 g (1¾ cups) **caster** (superfine) **sugar**
4 eggs
425 g (2 cups) **canned pumpkin purée**
175 g (1½ cups) **chopped walnuts**
melted white chocolate and roasted pumpkin seeds, to decorate (optional)

Preheat the oven to 180°C/350°F/Gas Mark 4.

Grease the cake pan with butter and line with parchment paper.

Sift together the flour, salt, soda and spices into a bowl.

Beat together the oil, sugar and eggs in another bowl, then mix in the pumpkin purée and 120 ml (½ cup) water.

Fold in the dry ingredients and the walnuts.

Pour into the prepared cake pan and bake for about 1 hour, until a knife inserted into the middle comes out clean.

Remove from the oven and let cool completely in the cake pan, then turn out.

At Rose Bakery, we drizzle some melted white chocolate over the top the cake and sprinkle with a few roasted pumpkin seeds.

{ Pumpkin Cake }

PURPLE CORN & BLUEBERRY CAKE

Purple corn powder is a rich source of powerful antioxidants and when my daughter introduced it to me from her health clinic, I decided to incorporate it into one of my cakes to see what it might bring, apart from the health benefits (see page 12). We first tried it in muffins, resulting a dull greyish-coloured muffin of no real interest. So then we thought of blueberries and not sifting it in with the flour, but rather swirling it in. So that is how this cake was created... Purple corn powder can be found in some health food stores and on the internet.

Makes 1 x 23 cm (9 inch) round or 1 x 24 x 9 cm (9 x 4 inch) rectangular cake

200 g (scant 1 cup) **butter, softened, plus extra for greasing**
175 g (scant 1 cup) **golden caster** (superfine) **sugar**
few drops vanilla extract
3 eggs
275 g (2½ cups) **plain** (all-purpose) **flour or half plain** (all-purpose) **and half wholemeal** (whole wheat) **flour**
2 teaspoons baking powder
½ teaspoon bicarbonate of soda (baking soda)
½ teaspoon salt
8 tablespoons plain yogurt
about 3 tablespoons purple corn powder
250 g (1 pint) **blueberries**
reduced blueberry jam, to decorate (optional)

Preheat the oven to 180°C/350°F/Gas Mark 4.

Grease the cake pan with butter and line with parchment paper.

Beat together the butter, sugar and vanilla with an electric mixer until pale, then beat in the eggs, one at a time.

Sift together the flour, baking powder, soda and salt into another bowl, then carefully fold it in, alternating with the yogurt, until well mixed.

Swirl in the purple corn powder and blueberries, but do not overmix.

Pour into the prepared cake pan and bake for about 45 minutes, until a knife inserted into the middle comes out clean.

Remove from the oven and let cool completely in the cake pan. Turn out and serve plain or glaze the top with reduced blueberry jam.

WHOLEMEAL (WHOLE WHEAT) & WALNUT CAKE

This has to be one of my favourite cakes because of its strong taste of walnuts, emphasized, oddly, by the addition of some almond-flavoured Amaretto liqueur. If you don't have any, honey or maple syrup will be good too.

Makes 1 x 30 x 7 cm (12 x 3 inch) rectangular cake

250 g (2¼ cups) **ground walnuts**
300 g (2¾ cups) **ground almonds**
120 g (1 cup) **wholemeal** (whole wheat) **flour**
1 teaspoon baking powder
½ teaspoon salt
350 g (1½ cups) **butter, softened, plus extra for greasing**
280 g (1⅓ cups) **golden caster** (superfine) **sugar**
5 eggs
120 ml (½ cup) **Amaretto liqueur**
icing (confectioners') **sugar or glazed whole walnuts, to decorate**

Preheat the oven to 180°C/350°F/Gas Mark 4.

Grease a rectangular cake pan with butter and line with parchment paper.

Put the walnuts, almonds, flour, baking powder and salt into a bowl and mix well.

Beat together the butter and sugar in another bowl until pale, then beat in the eggs, one at a time, until thoroughly mixed.

Fold in the dry ingredients and the amaretto and carefully mix together.

Pour into the prepared cake pan and bake for 50–60 minutes, until a knife inserted into the middle comes out clean.

Remove from the oven and let cool completely in the cake pan.

Turn out and serve simply with a dusting of icing sugar or whole glazed walnuts.

{ Purple Corn & Blueberry Cake }

{ Classic Genoise Sponge Cake }

CLASSIC GENOISE SPONGE CAKE

This is the simplest of cakes and the recipe we use for our Victoria sponge cake. It works for all light summer cakes, especially when red fruits come into season. We cut the cake in half and fill it generously with sweetened whipped cream, then add some berries, replace the top and lightly dust it with icing (confectioners') sugar and decorate with more cream and berries.

Makes 1 x 23 cm (9 inch) round cake

25 g (2 tablespoons) **butter, melted, plus extra for greasing**
4 eggs
120 g (⅔ cup) **caster** (superfine) **sugar**
120 g (1 cup) **plain** (all-purpose) **flour, sifted**
pinch of salt
few drops of vanilla extract

Preheat the oven to 180°C/350°F/Gas Mark 4.

Grease the cake pan with butter and line with parchment paper.

Using an electric mixer, beat the eggs with the sugar in a very clean mixing bowl for about 10 minutes, until very light and pale.

Carefully fold in the flour and salt, then gently fold in the melted butter and vanilla extract without deflating the mixture.

Pour into the prepared cake pan and bake for about 25–30 minutes, until a knife inserted into the middle comes out clean.

Turn out onto a wire rack and let cool.

SPONGE FINGERS

These simple biscuits (cookies), also known as *biscuits à la cuillère*, can be eaten as they are or used in cold desserts such as trifles and charlottes. They can be dipped in chocolate or served as an accompaniment to compotes of fruit. I love them simply by themselves, as they were once eaten in the French court in the fifteenth century.

Makes about 20

80 g (scant ½ cup) **caster** (superfine) **sugar**
3 large (US extra large) **eggs, separated**
few drops of vanilla extract
pinch of salt
80 g (¾ cup) **plain** (all-purpose) **flour, sifted**
50 g (½ cup) **icing** (confectioners') **sugar, sifted**

Preheat the oven to 180°C/350°F/Gas Mark 4.

Line a baking sheet with parchment paper.

Reserve 1 tablespoon of the caster sugar, then, using an electric mixer, beat the egg yolks with the remaining sugar on medium speed until very light, thick and pale in colour. Add the vanilla extract.

Whisk the egg whites with the salt in a grease-free bowl until stiff, then whisk in the reserved sugar.

Fold the sifted flour into the egg yolk mixture, alternating with the egg whites. Do not overmix, as you will knock out the air.

Spoon the mixture into a piping (pastry) bag fitted with a 1 cm (½ inch) plain nozzle (tip) and pipe it onto the prepared baking sheet in 7 cm (2¾ inch) lengths, spaced 2 cm (¾ inch) apart.

Sprinkle lightly with the icing sugar.

Bake for 12–15 minutes, until pale brown in colour.

Remove from the oven and transfer to a wire rack to cool. These biscuits can be stored in an airtight container for up to 2 weeks.

CHOCOLATE & ORANGE POLENTA CAKE

Having made our lemon polenta cake so often, we thought we might try a change and came up with the idea of the winning combination, orange and chocolate. And so this gluten-free cake came about, which is just as popular.

Makes 1 x 23 x 9 cm (9 x 4 inch) rectangular cake

225 g (1 cup) **butter, softened, plus extra for greasing**
100 ml (scant ½ cup) **double** (heavy) **cream**
60 g (2¼ ounces) **dark** (semisweet) **chocolate, chopped**
4 tablespoons unsweetened cocoa powder, plus extra for dusting (optional)
2 tablespoons hot water
200 g (1 cup) **golden caster** (superfine) **sugar**
3 eggs
few drops of vanilla extract
grated zest of 2 large oranges
275 g (2½ cups) **ground almonds**
5 tablespoons rice flour or cornmeal
70 g (½ cup) **polenta**
½ teaspoon salt
ganache, to serve (optional)

Preheat the oven to 180°C/350°F/Gas Mark 4.

Grease the cake pan with butter and line with parchment paper.

Pour the cream into a heatproof bowl and set over a pan of barely simmering water. When it is hot, add the chocolate, remove from the heat and let melt, then beat with a fork to blend well.

Mix the unsweetened cocoa powder with the hot water to make a thick paste in a small bowl, then stir into the cream and chocolate mixture.

Using an electric mixer, beat together the butter and sugar until pale, then beat in the eggs, one at a time, until thoroughly combined.

Beat in the vanilla, orange zest and chocolate mixture on a lower speed, then fold in the almonds, rice flour or cornmeal, polenta and salt.

Pour into the prepared cake pan and bake for about 45 minutes, until a knife inserted into the middle comes out clean. (Be careful not overcook this cake; it is really difficult to tell when it is done because so dark.)

Remove from the oven and let cool in the cake pan.

Turn out and serve it plain, dusted with unsweetened cocoa powder or decorated with ganache (a glaze of more melted chocolate and cream).

GREEN TEA GENOISE

This is a very light cake that has the soft taste of matcha green tea. It is delicious on its own, but it's even better served with a spoonful of crème fraîche and a red fruit compote or jam. Matcha is a top-quality green tea that has been very finely ground and is not the same as green tea powder. It is available from Japanese food stores.

Makes 1 x 28 cm (11 inch) cake

6 eggs, separated
100 g (½ cup) **caster** (superfine) **sugar**
4 tablespoons sunflower oil, plus extra for brushing
150 g (1¼ cups) **plain** (all-purpose) **flour, sifted**
2 tablespoons matcha green tea
2 egg whites
icing (confectioners') **sugar, for dusting**

Preheat the oven to 180°C/350°F/Gas Mark 4.

Brush the cake pan with oil and line with parchment paper.

Beat the yolks with 2 tablespoons of the sugar until pale, then beat in the oil, followed by 4 tablespoons water. Beat until thoroughly mixed and until it has the consistency of mayonnaise.

Fold in the flour and green tea with a spoon and mix well.

Whisk all the egg whites in a grease-free bowl until soft peaks form. Gradually add the remaining caster sugar, whisking well after each addition, until firm and glossy.

Gently fold into the green tea mixture in 2 batches to avoid knocking out the air.

Pour into the prepared cake pan and bake for about 35 minutes, until a knife inserted in the middle comes out clean.

Turn out onto a wire rack and let cool.

Dust with icing sugar before serving.

{ Green Tea Genoise }

{ Welsh Tea Cakes }

WELSH TEA CAKES

These are so delicious when served warm straight from the griddle (grill pan), and make a nice change from warm scones and jam.

Makes about 10

225 g (2 cups) **self-raising flour, plus extra for dusting**
1 teaspoon mixed (pumpkin pie) **spice or ground allspice**
pinch of salt
80 g (scant ½ cup) **caster** (superfine) **sugar, plus extra for sprinkling**
100 g (7 tablespoons) **butter**
80 g (⅓ cup) **currants or 80 g** (⅔ cup) **sultanas** (golden raisins)
grated zest of 1 lemon
1 large (US extra large) **egg, beaten**
1 tablespoon milk (optional)

Sift together the flour, spice and salt into a bowl and stir in the sugar.

Add the butter and rub in with your fingertips until the mixture looks like breadcrumbs.

Stir in the dried fruit and lemon zest, then pour in the egg and mix with a fork until the mixture comes together like pastry dough. If it is too dry, add the milk.

Roll out on a lightly floured surface to about 5 mm (¼ inch) thick and stamp out 4 cm (1½ inch) rounds with a cutter.

Heat a griddle (grill pan), heavy frying pan or skillet to medium hot.

Add the tea cakes and cook for 3–4 minutes on each side, until golden.

Sprinkle with extra sugar and serve immediately.

{ Semolina Pudding }

Puddings

As well our cakes, we always have at least one pudding on the menu. They are the thing that people remember when they leave – comfort food completely. These recipes are based on traditional recipes and eggs are essential as setting agents for the cream and custard, and for the meringues of course.

SEMOLINA PUDDING

Memories of school dinners often cause this pudding to be greeted with groans, but made properly, it is delicious.

Serves 8

120 g (½ cup) **butter, softened, plus extra for greasing**
1 litre (4¼ cups) **milk**
200 g (1 cup) **caster** (superfine) **sugar**
grated zest of 3 oranges
few drops of vanilla extract
pinch of salt
130 g (¾ cup) **semolina**
5 eggs, beaten

For the orange syrup

250 ml (1 cup) **fresh orange juice**
grated zest of ½ orange, cut into thin strips
150 g (¾ cup) **caster** (superfine) **sugar**
1 cinnamon stick

Preheat the oven to 180°C/350°F/Gas Mark 4.

Grease a 2 litre (8½ cup) square ovenproof dish with butter.

Pour the milk into a pan, add the sugar, orange zest, vanilla and salt and bring just to a boil.

Reduce the heat and pour in the semolina in a steady stream, whisking constantly. Stir with the whisk or a wooden spoon until well thickened and smooth.

Remove the pan from the heat and stir in the butter until melted.

Beat in the eggs, then pour into the prepared dish and bake for about 35 minutes, until set.

Meanwhile, make the orange syrup. Put all the ingredients into a small pan and cook over low heat until the sugar is dissolved. Increase to medium heat and boil for about 8 minutes, until thick and syrupy.

Remove and discard the cinnamon stick, pour the syrup into a little sauce boat and serve on the side or poured over the semolina pudding.

This pudding is best served warm, but is also great cold.

BREAD & BUTTER PUDDING

At Rose Bakery we use *panettone*, a wonderful Italian fruit bread, but if this is not available, use any good-quality, crustless fruit bread. It is essential that the bread will soak up practically all the custard, so you have a pudding that feels like one, not just a custard with bits of bread as a topping!

Serves 6

80 g (6 tablespoons) **butter, plus extra
  for greasing**
5–6 slices panettone or fruit loaf
500 ml (2¼ cups) **full-fat** (whole) **milk or half milk
  and half single** (light) **cream**
grated zest of 1 lemon
grated zest of 1 orange
60 g (⅓ cup) **caster** (superfine) **sugar**
pinch of salt
few drops of vanilla extract
3 eggs
3 egg yolks
reduced apricot jam, to glaze (optional)

Lightly grease an ovenproof dish with butter.

Put the slices of bread in the oven for 5–10 minutes, until lightly toasted, then remove, spread generously with butter and cut in half. Arrange them evenly in the prepared dish.

Pour the milk into a pan, add the lemon and orange zest, sugar, salt and vanilla and heat gently until just hot but not boiling, then remove from the heat.

Lightly beat together the eggs and egg yolks in a bowl, then pour the hot milk over them, whisking well. Strain into a jug (pitcher) and pour the custard over the bread. Let stand for about 35 minutes to soak up the liquid.

Meanwhile, preheat the oven to 180°C/350°F/ Gas Mark 4.

Put the dish in a roasting pan, pour in warm water to come about halfway up the sides and bake for about 35 minutes, until the sides are puffing up and the middle is just set.

Remove from the oven and serve while still warm. We sometimes glaze the top with reduced apricot jam.

If you are using brown bread instead of fruit loaf, slightly increase the quantity of sugar. Spread the buttered bread with a little jam or marmalade and top the pudding with demerara (turbinado) sugar. Just as nice.

DEEP CUSTARD TARTS

I love this tart as it is not too sweet and it satisfies a taste for crunchiness and creaminess without being too rich. Tarts like this are so hard to find nowadays unless you are lucky enough to have an old-fashioned bakery nearby. So why not make one yourself?

You will need individual deep tart pans, or, failing that, you can always use muffin pans which are also quite deep. We use our Basic Pastry Dough recipe (see page 65) with 1 tablespoon caster (superfine) sugar included in the dry ingredients as the pastry base for these tarts. Any shortcrust pastry (basic pie dough) will work as long as it is not a sweet pastry, but rather dry, crisp and savoury.

Makes 8 tarts

3 eggs
3 egg yolks
1 teaspoon cornflour (cornstarch) **(optional)**
300 ml (1¼ cups) **milk**
200 ml (scant 1 cup) **single** (light) **cream**
1 vanilla pod (bean) **or 1 teaspoon vanilla extract**
60 g (⅓ cup) **caster** (superfine) **sugar**
pinch of salt
pinch of grated nutmeg or ground cinnamon
8 x 10 cm (4 inch) **pastry cases** (shells)**, baked
  blind (see page 65)**

Preheat the oven to 150°C/300°F/Gas Mark 2.

Beat together the eggs, egg yolks and cornflour, if using, in a bowl.

Heat the milk and cream with the vanilla, sugar and salt to just below boiling point, then remove from the heat and pour onto the eggs, whisking constantly.

Strain the custard into a jug (pitcher) or bowl and pour it into the tart cases.

Sprinkle with the nutmeg or cinnamon and bake for about 30 minutes, until the filling is just set.

Serve warm or cold simply as they are, there's no need for any garnish.

{ Deep Custard Tarts }

SOY CRÈME CARAMEL

We are frequently asked for dairy-free options at Rose Bakery, and this version of a classic dessert works really well.

Serves 6

300 g (1½ cups) **caster** (superfine) **sugar**
1 litre (4¼ cups) **soy milk**
grated zest of 1 lemon
1 vanilla pod (bean)
3 eggs
6 egg yolks
pinch of salt

Preheat the oven to 150°C/300°F/Gas Mark 2.

Put 150 g (¾ cup) of the sugar and 4 tablespoons water into a heavy pan and cook over high heat, gently swirling the pan until the sugar dissolves, then boil, without stirring, for 4–5 minutes until a golden caramel forms. Immediately remove from the heat and divide the caramel among 6 individual ramekins or pour it into a single large ovenproof dish. Let it set.

Pour the soy milk into a pan, add the lemon zest and vanilla pod and bring to just below boiling point, then remove the pan from the heat and remove the vanilla pod.

Slit the vanilla pod and scrape the seeds into the milk mixture.

Beat together the eggs, egg yolks, the remaining sugar and the salt in a bowl, then gradually add the warm soy milk, whisking constantly. Strain into a jug (pitcher).

Pour the custard over the set caramel and stand the ramekins or dish in a roasting pan. Pour in warm water to come halfway up the sides, cover with foil and bake for about 45 minutes, until just set but slightly wobbly in the middle.

Remove from the oven and let cool, then chill in the refrigerator for a few hours, preferably overnight.

Turn out onto individual plates or a serving plate, pour the caramel over the top and serve.

ORANGE CRÈME CARAMEL

This classic never fails to please. It can be made in a single dish or several ramekins.

Serves 6

500 ml (generous 2 cups) **full-cream** (whole) **milk or half milk and half single** (light) **cream**
230 g (1¼ cup) **caster** (superfine) **sugar**
pinch of salt
grated zest of 4 oranges
3 eggs
3 egg yolks

Pour the milk into a pan, add 80 g (scant ½ cup) of the sugar and the salt and bring just to a boil.

Add the orange zest, remove the pan from the heat and let stand for at least 1 hour.

Beat the eggs in a bowl, pour in the flavoured milk and mix well without frothing.

To make the caramel, put the remaining sugar into a pan, pour in just enough water to cover – about 4 tablespoons – and bring to a boil over high heat, gently swirling the pan occasionally until the sugar has dissolved. Cook, without stirring, until a lovely golden-brown caramel has formed.

Remove from the heat, pour into an ovenproof dish or divide among individual ramekins and let set.

Meanwhile, preheat the oven to 150°C/300°F/Gas Mark 2.

Strain the orange custard through a fine strainer over the set caramel and put the dish or ramekins into a roasting pan.

Pour in warm water to come about halfway up the sides and bake for about 1 hour if using a single dish or 45 minutes if using ramekins, until just set but still with a slight wobble in the middle.

Remove from the oven and let stand in the bain-marie until cold, then chill in the refrigerator for at least 6 hours.

When ready to serve, run a round-bladed knife around the side and invert onto a serving dish or individual plates. Perfection.

{ Orange Crème Caramel }

A SIMPLE APPLE FLAN

Since this dessert is so simple, you have to use the best-flavoured apples that disintegrate when cooked, such as Bramleys in England or possibly the Canada gris in France. This is only possible in the winter months when they have the best flavour.

Serves 6

150 g (¾ cup) **caster** (superfine) **sugar**
juice of 1 lemon
60 g (4½ tablespoons) **butter**
1 kg (2¼ pounds) **apples**
3 eggs, beaten
1 tablespoon cornflour (cornstarch)
Crème Anglaise (see page 120), to serve
  (optional)

Put 100 g (½ cup) of the sugar and 2 tablespoons water into a heavy pan and cook over high heat, gently swirling the pan until the sugar dissolves, then boil, without stirring, for 4–5 minutes until a golden caramel forms.

Immediately remove from the heat, add half the lemon juice and 25 g (2 tablespoons) of the butter and mix well.

Pour into a round ovenproof dish to cover the base and set aside.

Peel, core and slice the apples, put them into a stainless steel pan, add the remaining lemon juice and cook over low heat until they have softened and turned into a thick purée.

Stir in the remaining sugar, or enough to taste.

Remove the pan from the heat and stir in the beaten eggs, the remaining butter and the cornflour.

Pour the apple mixture over the caramel and bake for about 30 minutes, until slightly firm.

Remove from the oven and let cool, then chill in the refrigerator overnight.

Just before turning out, place on low heat for a few minutes to release the caramel.

This flan is delicious served with crème anglaise.

ROSE BAKERY CHOCOLATE MOUSSE

This is a classic chocolate mousse that is not too sweet. It needs a very good-quality dark (semisweet) chocolate. We use Valrhona 72 per cent which always gives that perfect, rounded bitterness I like.

Serves 6–7

300 g (11 ounces) **dark** (semisweet) **chocolate,**
  broken into pieces
175 ml (¾ cup) **double** (heavy) **cream**
6 eggs, separated
1–2 tablespoons caster (superfine) **sugar**
3 tablespoons hot espresso coffee
1 tablespoon whisky, dark rum or Grand Marnier
chocolate beads, to decorate (optional)

Melt the chocolate in a heatproof bowl set over a pan of barely simmering water, then remove from the heat.

Meanwhile, whip the cream until soft peaks form.

Beat the egg whites in another grease-free bowl until soft peaks form, then add the sugar and continue beating for a few more minutes.

Beat the egg yolks well, then beat in the hot espresso and whisky, rum or Grand Marnier.

Stir in the melted chocolate. The mixture will thicken a lot and become almost unmanageable. To lighten it, add half the egg whites and fold in, then fold in the cream.

Finally, fold in the rest of the egg whites, being careful not to overmix. In fact, I quite like the marbled effect when the mix is not perfectly combined.

Turn into a serving bowl or individual dishes and chill in the refrigerator for at least 1 hour before serving.

Serve plain or decorated, according to taste. At Rose Bakery we sprinkle chocolate beads on top.

PAVLOVA

Making meringue is such a satisfying process and a good way to use up all those egg whites that we put aside. It's an awful shame to throw away bowls of egg whites left over from making custards and other desserts that require only yolks, so making meringue is really cheering.

Serves 8

8 egg whites
pinch of salt
450 g (2¼ cups) **caster** (superfine) **sugar**
dash of vanilla extract
1 teaspoon cream of tartar (optional)
1 litre (4¼ cups) **double** (heavy) **cream**
fruit, to decorate (see method)

Preheat the oven to 120°C/250°F/Gas Mark ½.

Line a baking sheet with parchment paper.

Beat the egg whites with the salt in a spotlessly clean metal bowl until firm.

Gradually drizzle in the sugar, beating constantly at medium speed until very firm and glossy.

Add the vanilla and fold in the cream of tartar, if using. (Cream of tartar is intended to add more volume and stabilize the meringue, but I don't think it's really necessary.)

Spoon the mixture onto the prepared baking sheet and form into a large round, then bake for about 1 hour, until slightly crisp on the outside but soft inside.

Remove from the oven and leave to cool, then transfer the meringue to a serving dish.

Whip the cream until it forms soft peaks, then spread it on top of the meringue base with a spatula.

Top with any fruit you like. Our favourites are red berries, passion fruit, mango, bananas or poached apricots. In winter we use the following combinations instead of soft fruits:

– Chestnut purée and melted dark (semisweet) chocolate
– Apple purée and caramel
– Banana, lime zest and caramel
– Poached pear and dark (semisweet) chocolate
– Poached peaches and almonds

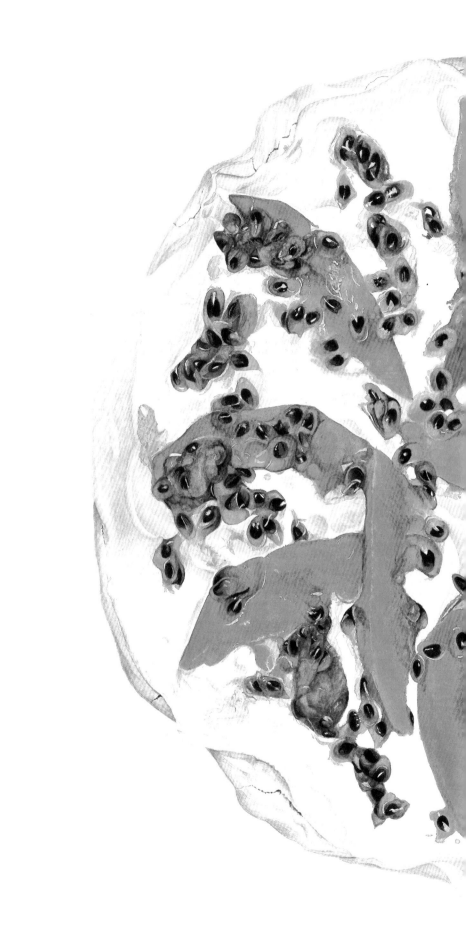

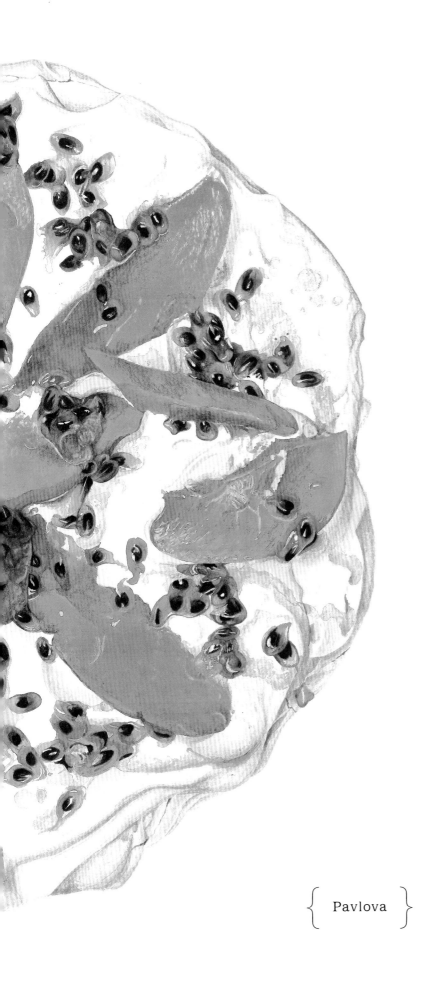

{ Pavlova }

{ Eton Mess }

ETON MESS

Traditionally served at the annual picnic on 4 June at England's famous Eton College, this 'mess' is a fabulous mixture of crushed meringue, whipped cream and fresh strawberries.

Serves 6–8

8 egg whites
pinch of salt
450 g (2¼ cups) **caster** (superfine) **sugar**
dash of vanilla extract
1 teaspoon cream of tartar (optional)
1 litre (4¼ cups) **double** (heavy) **cream**
1 kg (2¼ pounds) **strawberries or other berries,**
  sliced or lightly crushed

Preheat the oven to 120°C/250°F/Gas Mark ½.

Line a baking sheet with parchment paper.

Beat the egg whites with the salt in a spotlessly clean metal bowl until firm.

Gradually drizzle in the sugar, beating constantly at medium speed until very firm and glossy.

Add the vanilla and fold in the cream of tartar, if using. (Cream of tartar is intended to add more volume and stabilize the meringue, but I don't think it's really necessary.)

Using a large spoon, drop big heaps of the mixture onto the prepared baking tray and bake for 2–3 hours, until crisp on the outside but slightly gooey inside.

Remove from the oven and let cool.

Whip the cream, then add the meringues, crush them and fold together with the cream.

Add the strawberries or your choice of soft fruits and stir until the 'mess' is achieved. (We usually use a mixture of strawberries, raspberries and blueberries.)

ÎLES FLOTTANTES

This is the ultimate egg dessert for sure, and a big favourite of my partner, Jean-Charles. We don't make it often enough as far as he is concerned. Some people add praline, almonds or other toasted nuts on top, but I prefer this simple version.

Serves 6

For the meringues

6 large (US extra large) **egg whites**
pinch of salt
dash of lemon juice
140 g (⅔ cup) **caster** (superfine) **sugar**
few drops of vanilla extract
400 ml (1¾ cups) **milk**
400 ml (1¾ cups) **single** (light) **cream**

For the crème anglaise

8 egg yolks
65 g (⅓ cup) **caster** (superfine) **sugar**
few drops of vanilla extract

For the caramel

225 g (generous 1 cup) **caster** (superfine) **sugar**

Whisk the egg whites with the salt and lemon juice in a grease-free metal bowl until they are almost stiff. Add the sugar and continue whisking and finally add the vanilla.

Heat the milk and cream in a pan until just simmering. Shape the meringue into quenelles with 2 tablespoons, gently drop them into the milk mixture, cover and simmer in batches, carefully turning once, for about 10 minutes.

Using a slotted spoon, lift out the meringues onto a plate and chill. Reserve the milk mixture.

To make the crème anglaise, bring the reserved milk and cream mixture just to a boil in a pan, then remove from the heat.

Beat the egg yolks with the sugar and vanilla in a bowl, then pour in the hot milk and mix well.

Pour the milk mixture back into the pan and cook over low heat, stirring constantly with a wooden spoon, until the custard thickens slightly and coats the spoon. Strain into a jug (pitcher), let cool and chill in the refrigerator. (You can add a teaspoon of brandy or some vanilla seeds if you like.)

To make the caramel, put the sugar into a pan, add 4 tablespoons water and bring to a boil over high heat, gently swirling the pan until the sugar has dissolved, then cook, without stirring, until it forms a deep-coloured caramel.

Remove from the heat and add another 4 tablespoons water, standing well back and protecting your arms, as it will splutter furiously.

Return the pan to low heat for a few minutes to make sure the caramel is smooth, then remove from the heat and set aside.

Divide the crème anglaise among individual serving bowls and place the meringues on top to float. Drizzle the caramel over the top. Perfect.

{ Îles Flottantes }

INDEX

Page numbers in italics refer to the illustrations

{ Green Tarts }

{ Hen's Egg }

{ Egg Shell }

Afterword

These are just a few of the many hundreds of ways you can
eat eggs whether they are served simply on their own, the
main ingredient of a dish or part of a more complex recipe.
They feature in recipes from all continents and are as
important in contemporary cooking as in classic cuisine.
A multitude of books have been written extolling their virtues
and versatility. I just love eating them simply. Whenever
I eat eggs there is always a sense of extreme satisfaction that
I have eaten something so simple but special, nourishing
and generous. A perfect food.

Acknowledgements

An enormous thank you to Fiona for her exquisite paintings; once again to all the staff at Phaidon, especially Victoria and Laurence for their patience and knowledge, and particularly to Rosie for shepherding this project through, to Frith for her intuitive design and Patrick. This book looks and feels exactly as I had hoped. Many thanks to all my staff at Rose Bakery in Paris, London, Tokyo and Seoul. And a special mention to Tomoko who has worked wonders in Japan.

This is for Rufus and Elijah with love.

PARIS

LONDON

TOKYO

SEOUL

{ Rose Bakery }

Phaidon Press Limited
Regent's Wharf
All Saints Street
London N1 9PA

Phaidon Press Inc.
180 Varick Street
New York, NY 10014

www.phaidon.com

First published 2013
© 2013 Phaidon Press Limited

ISBN 978 0 7148 6241 5

A CIP catalogue record for this book is available
from the British Library.

Illustrations by Fiona Strickland
Designed by Studio Frith

Printed in China

MERCI
AND
THANK YOU

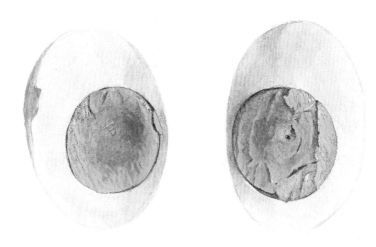